LIGHTPOSTS
FOR LIVING

LIGHTPOSTS
FOR LIVING

THE ART OF CHOOSING A JOYFUL LIFE

THOMAS KINKADE
WITH ANNE CHRISTIAN BUCHANAN

WARNER BOOKS

A TIME WARNER COMPANY

For my family

Warner Books, Inc., 1271 Avenue of the Americas, New York, NY 10020

A Time Warner Company

Printed in the United States of America

First Printing April 1999

10 9 8 7 6 5 4 3 2 1

Library of Congress Cataloging-in-Publication Data

Kinkade, Thomas
    Lightposts for living: the art of choosing a joyful life/Thomas
Kinkade; with Anne Christian Buchanan
        p. cm.
    ISBN 0-446-52522-7
    1. Conduct of life. 2. Joy. I. Buchanan, Anne Christian.
II. Title
BJ1581.2.K493   1999
170'.44--DC21   98-41617
                                                              CIP

CONTENTS

INTRODUCTION: A SHINING LIFE...VII

LIGHTPOST 1 THE COLOR OF JOY...1
Living in the Light of Abiding Happiness

LIGHTPOST 2 GETTING LITTLE *Living in a Playful Light*...17

LIGHTPOST 3 A PICTURE OF HARMONY *Living in a Balanced Light*...35

LIGHTPOST 4 THE ABUNDANCE OF ENOUGH *Living in the Light of Simplicity*...55

LIGHTPOST 5 FILTERED SUNSHINE *Living in a Positive Light*...77

LIGHTPOST 6 A NECESSARY BEAUTY *Living in the Light of the Lovely*...93

LIGHTPOST 7 A GLOWING HEARTH *Living Close to the Warm Light of Home*...111

LIGHTPOST 8 A SERVANT'S HEART *Living in a Selfless Light*...133

LIGHTPOST 9 SAYING GRACE *Living in the Light of Thankfulness*...151

LIGHTPOST 10 A RADIANT SUNRISE *Living in a Romantic Light*...171

LIGHTPOST 11 LIGHT A FRESH CANDLE *Living in the Light of Creativity*...189

LIGHTPOST 12 VOYAGING TOWARD DAWN
Living in the Light of Unfolding Miracles...211

AFTERWORD: LET YOUR LIGHT SHINE...231

SOURCES OF LIGHT...235

A SHINING LIFE

He that has light within his own clear breast
May sit i' th' centre and enjoy bright day.
— JOHN MILTON

Close your eyes, and picture a place you're yearning to be.

A place that is beautiful and comforting, where everything seems hopeful and alive. A garden, perhaps, or a rustic cabin nestled beside a mountain stream. A pristine beach kissed gold by the sunset. A meandering path by an ocean. A cozy cottage warmed by the presence of people you love.

Picture a world the way it was meant to be. Where work and leisure take their proper place, where faith and hope and love abide and new possibilities forever blossom. Where families and friendships flourish and there's time to savor the myriad moments that make up a life lived to the fullest.

This is life the way you're hungry to live it, the way as a child you dreamed it could be, the way you still believe it can be in your deepest heart of hearts. A life that shines with wonder and beauty and joy and faith — all the qualities that make life truly worthwhile.

Sound wonderful? It does to me, too. That's exactly the kind of life, in fact, that I try to evoke through my art.

In more than twenty years as a professional painter, my consistent goal has been to create inviting worlds that draw people into their depths and encourage them to seek a better, brighter, more hopeful existence. In the process, I have given much thought to the specific qualities that make life good and the visual attributes that evoke a joyful way of living. And through all my years of experimenting with pictorial techniques, through hundreds of excursions into the deepest places of my imagination, I have found that one visual characteristic more than any other embodies the peace and tranquillity we all yearn for. That characteristic is *light*.

Light, I have found, is a profoundly evocative force within a painting, at once energizing and calming. Canvases that glow with radiant, transcendent light seem to invite the viewer in and allow him or her to feel comfortable and at home within the scene depicted. They have the power to inspire people with hope and reaffirm their deepest yearnings.

My own paintings, even after weeks of work and preparation, can seem almost dull and mundane until the joyful moment when I take brush in hand and begin to "turn on the lights"—adding the luminous highlights in the lampposts that line a village lane or brushing a delicate wash of golden white to enliven a sky. Each sparkling sunshine accent that pierces a cloud or dapples a lawn, each gentle gleam from a radiant, hearth-lit window lights the way into the luminous world within the painting.

For me, this process of adding light to a canvas is the most exciting stage in the development of a painting. To see a picture emerge from the shadowy depths into the brilliance of light is an amazing and even miraculous experience. Although based on careful planning—I usually know from the first brushstroke how I want to develop the effects of light in a painting, and I work hard to lay a foundation that will allow the light to shine—it also has a lot to do with spontaneity and faith. As I work, I often feel as though the hand guiding the brushwork is not my own, as though a special point of contact is being established with the divine. Sometimes my work feels almost like a form of worship.

Stroke by stroke, then, the light begins to emerge. And only then will the painting begin to match the original vision I saw in my heart. Only then will it begin to take on a joyous life of its own, to acquire the inviting radiance that draws people into its depths.

"I want to live there," collectors will often tell me at a gallery or show. They seem drawn to the light-filled worlds in my canvases. I believe this is because human beings instinctively crave a light-filled existence.

Don't you? Don't you feel drawn to glowing hearths, flickering campfires, old-fashioned lamplight? Aren't you pulled irresistibly outdoors on a day when the sun shines golden or a night when the full moon bathes the world in silver? And don't you crave a life that radiates light—that overflows with the same clarity and warmth and sparkling joy that light in nature suggests to us?

Seeking light is one of the most basic and universal human impulses. Biologically speaking, we hunger for light, leaning toward its warmth and brightness like a green plant on a windowsill. Our skin absorbs essential vitamin D from sunlight. Our eyes need proper lighting to remain healthy. Without light, life itself would cease to exist. Just as surely as we gasp for oxygen or thirst for water, we look for light because we need it to survive.

Truly the light is sweet,
and a pleasant thing it is for the eyes to behold the sun.
— THE BOOK OF ECCLESIASTES

Emotionally, too, we gravitate toward light, seeking out sunlit spaces and illuminated corners, shying away from gloom. When we enter a darkened

room, we don't walk boldly in
and sit down, closing the door
behind us. Instead, we frantical-
ly search for the light switch,
shuffling our feet to avoid
obstacles until the room is illuminated. Outdoors, at night, we
gravitate to the pools of light
beneath street lamps and feel
comforted as we approach the
glowing windows of home.
Light eases anxiety, warms our
disposition, makes us feel safe
and secure.

Is it a surprise, then, that
images of light and darkness fill
our spiritual vocabularies as
well? Almost every religion,
every culture, finds meaning
and metaphor in stories of day and night, sunshine and shadow, the radiant
glow of goodness and the murky depths of evil. And almost all would agree
on the spiritual reality that mirrors our biological and emotional yearnings —
that light is better than darkness, that the things of light are better than the
things of darkness.

The specific interpretation of what this means, of course, will vary. And
yet the basic ingredients of a light-filled life remain obvious and universal.
They form the fundamental list of qualities most of us want for our lives. Love,
joy, contentment, hope, fulfillment, enthusiasm, and inner tranquillity are all
luminous characteristics of living in the light. Hatred, sorrow, discontent-
ment, hopelessness, lack of fulfillment, apathy, and inner turmoil represent
the effects of darkness. No matter what our background or beliefs, few would
argue that the first list is better than the second!

But with that basic agreement, of course, come inevitable questions.

If we agree that it is a good thing to "live in the light" — that is, better to
shine with love, joy, and peace than to lurk in the shadows of hatred, bitterness,
and strife — why do so many lives continue to be shrouded with darkness?

More to the point, if light is better than darkness, how do we get more light? Can we turn on the lights in our lives as simply as we turn on the lights in a dark room or as easily as I, with a few quick brushstrokes, can begin to turn on the lights in an almost-complete painting?

Well, people are more complicated than paintings. And yet I believe that adding light to the canvas of our daily existence is a simpler process than we often make it out to be. I believe it really is possible to think and act in ways that shine more radiant joy into our lives and the lives of those around us.

Within the pages of this book I will attempt to "illuminate" some of these steps to a brighter existence.

Though simple, these steps are crucial to achieving what I like to call the "lifestyle of light," a quality of living that, ideally at least, is unhindered by dark forces of negativity, overstress, and despair. As the complexities and demands of my life have increased, these principles of light-filled living have time and again held back the darkness of stress, discontent, and imbalance.

This is my inspiration for writing a book of this sort. Although my life as a committed husband, the father of four, an artist, and a cofounder of a large public corporation may on the surface seem complex and demanding (as no doubt your life is as well), I have remained essentially a happy and balanced man. My life isn't perfect, but it is rich and enjoyable. I have fun. I spend both quality and quantity time with my family. I surround myself with what I love. The vision of simplicity and beauty that fills my paintings is also being fulfilled in my life. Or, to rephrase it, what I paint is what I try my best to live. And I know it is possible to live in the light because by necessity (and by much trial and error) I've learned to do just that.

This book, then, is my attempt to share a few of the things I've learned about the art of turning on the lights in a painting or in a life. My prayer is that the thoughts within these pages will provide both inspiration and practical help—to remind you that the shining life you crave is really possible and to suggest some simple ways to achieve it.

There's nothing complex or difficult here. There's nothing revolutionary or controversial. No special tools are required—just your thoughtfulness and your deep desire to turn up the lights in your life, to experience more joy and fulfillment in your day-to-day existence and live in a world more consistent with your deepest yearnings.

I hope these chapters will be for you like old-fashioned lightposts leading down a cobblestone path. Each illuminates a different aspect of the lifestyle of light—although unavoidably, because a well-lived life is seamless and connected, there will be some overlap of themes.

I hope, when all are added together, that the overall effect is bright indeed. At the very least, I trust that you will catch a brief glimpse of the light that lies waiting for you, even if at the end of the tunnel. And once you've "seen the light," I'm confident the darkness will daily grow less dark.

I believe a radiant, light-filled tomorrow should be normal to the experience of living. It is our birthright as human beings. I pray these pages will help you claim it for your own life.

LIGHTPOSTS
FOR LIVING

ONE

THE COLOR OF JOY

LIVING IN THE LIGHT OF
ABIDING HAPPINESS

Joy is the sweet voice, joy the luminous cloud—
We in ourselves rejoice!
And thence flows all that charms or ear or sight,
All melodies the echoes of that voice,
All colors a suffusion from that light.
— SAMUEL TAYLOR COLERIDGE

What color is a yellow chair?

For me as a painter, the answer is not quite as simple as it sounds.

I learned long ago that the *apparent* color of an object (the way it looks) is a very different thing from its *intrinsic* color (the color it really is).

In the fiery light of sunset, the yellow chair may reflect an orange glow. As daylight continues to fade, the color will fade as well. In the cool shadows of a tree-shaded lawn, the chair may take on a greenish hue or appear almost violet when silhouetted against a distant sunlit meadow.

And yet, if you move the chair back to a neutral light, you see that the intrinsic color of the chair has never really changed. Regardless of the external circumstances, a yellow chair is still a yellow chair.

Artists refer to the yellowness of that chair—the color it is no matter what the light—as its *local color*. Local color is the color that belongs to the basic chemistry or biology of the thing, that is not dependent on tricks of light or external modification. Outside forces may change its appearance, but not its essence.

That analogy helps me a lot when I think about my happiness.

After all, each of us wants to be happy. Given the choice, we'd prefer to live our entire lives in the golden light of fortunate circumstances. And we all have a mental list of what such happiness entails. What's on your list? A great job, a happy family, a life of adventure?

The problem, of course, is that none of us gets everything we think we want all the time. Some of us don't even get close. Others get what we yearned for and then find we don't want it anymore. And although we can exercise considerable influence on what happens around us, we can no more dictate our changing circumstances than I can tell the sunset to hold still while I attempt to capture its color on canvas.

Basing my happiness on what happens to me, then, is a little like depending on the ambient light to color an unpainted chair yellow. It might work for a while, but sooner or later the light, and the chair, will change. If I really want a yellow chair, therefore, I'll do well to invest in some brushes and a can or two of yellow paint!

And if I really want to be happy, I'd better realize that joy, as poet Don Blanding once put it, is an inside job. I need to cultivate a fundamental attitude of satisfaction and celebration that can keep on shining golden no matter how the light shifts around me. I need to concentrate on making sure that joy is the local color in my heart.

Maintaining that kind of durable joy isn't quite as simple as slapping a coat of paint on a chair, but it's not all that mysterious, either. Over the years I have discovered a number of strategies that help me keep my heart-attitude sparkling and tinted with joy.

CHOOSE YOUR COLOR

Before the strategies, however, comes the decision. At some deep level, consciously or unconsciously, you have to decide that you *want* to be joyful. You have to take a deep breath and trust that life, despite its ups and downs, is essentially wonderful, that the finished tapestry of your days will be a thing of beauty.

And yes, it *is* a leap of faith. Depending on your personality or your temperament or your philosophy or your current circumstances, it may feel like a *big* leap. If you are going through a time of pain or doubt, you may wonder if you can even make it. But you don't have to take that leap of faith like a trapeze artist swinging out over nothingness. It can feel, in fact, like taking a simple, small step in your chosen direction—the direction of happiness.

> *"And now you have joy?"*
> *"I do indeed."*
> *"And how did you get it?"*
> *"I chose it, admitted it into my life, then I celebrated its arrival in my heart.*
> *I made my celebration so loud and boisterous,*
> *I prohibited all gloom from attending the celebration."*
> —CALVIN MILLER

You take a step. You choose your color—decide that joy is the hue you want your heart to be. And then you start making the little and large choices that over time will paint your heart happy.

It really is possible to color a dark canvas golden, even with the tiniest of brushes. You just keep on dabbing the paint, and sooner or later you transform the surface with brightness. In the same way, if you keep on making joy-choices, small and large, your heart will eventually display a joyful tint that is more durable than you ever imagined.

GIVE YOURSELF A PERK

How do you make joyful choices?

On the very simplest level, you condition yourself for joy by doing little things you love on a regular basis.

I have long been in the habit of building joy-breaks into the course of my days—allowing myself certain small pleasures for the express purpose of keeping my

attitude bright. I like Luci Swindoll's term for these small indulgences: "perks."

One of my favorite perks during fair weather is to simply take a book out into the sunshine. After lunch I pull up a chair on my patio and spend ten minutes or so basking and browsing. The combination of the warm sun, the absorbing words, and the pure relaxation is almost guaranteed to lift my spirits and send me back to work with a higher joy-quotient.

Now, the thought of reading outdoors may do nothing for you. But how would you feel about a walk in the neighborhood park . . . or parking your car on a hilltop and enjoying the view . . . a chat with an old friend over coffee . . . lighting a candle and listening to fine music? Anything that builds a simple sense of pleasure or optimism can be effective in building up the base coat of happiness deep in your heart.

I should probably add at this point that I am not talking about selfish, self-destructive, or self-delusional behaviors. I'm not speaking of feeding your inner emptiness with a gallon of ice cream or bolstering your shaky self-esteem with an expensive afternoon at the mall, loading up debt on your credit cards. Such compulsive or addictive pursuits paint only a temporary wash of brass that tarnishes rapidly. Their end result is more pain, not more joy.

The good news, though, is that the world is absolutely brimming with simple forms of enjoyment that do no such harm. Even if you struggle with compulsive or addictive behavior in some areas of your life, you can still find countless ways to give yourself a perk without adding to your problems. I believe you'll find, in fact, that the very act of indulging yourself in simple, joy-building perks will make it easier for you to say no to the false joy of destructive pleasure.

Even if you haven't felt joyful in a long time, chances are you can think of at least one small pursuit that makes you smile, lightens your load, refreshes your spirit. If it is small and simple, why not do it today?

Don't let yourself be swayed by excuses. Don't let your hurried consciousness nag that you don't have time. Anyone can spare fifteen minutes a day for the practice of conscious joy. Above all, ignore the scolding inner voice that accuses you of being frivolous or selfish. Setting yourself up for joy is an investment, not an indulgence. Investing the necessary time and expense to build a joy-base in your heart will not only bless you; it will give you what you need to be a blessing to others who are themselves in need of a little joy.

*I think most of us look at personal delights as somewhere between
minimally important and borderline immoral.
We like them, but we're not sure we ought to.
We seldom give them a high priority when other demands
are competing for our attention.
Nevertheless, the soul feeds on simple joys and withers without them.*
— VICTORIA MORAN

LOOK FOR SURPRISES

In addition to your deliberately planned perks, don't forget to watch for surprises. You never know what unplanned encounter will rescue a dreary day and add a solid brushstroke of joy to your heart.

The other day, for instance, I discovered a spot in my neighborhood I had never seen before. Choosing a slightly different route for my daily exercise, I came upon a wonderful little oasis of garden, lawn, trees, even a little footbridge — a carefully tended snippet of paradise. The gift of this discovery was

a real delight. I returned from my walk with my joy-quotient bolstered.

The potential for such joyful surprises lurks around every corner of almost every day. A funny remark from a child, a spectacular cloud formation, a tree full of butterflies, a fresh breeze on a hot day, or just a simple, unexpected sense that all is well — any of these small experiences can be a gift of joy if you let yourself receive it. But in the rush of schedules and responsibilities and even recreational pursuits, it becomes far too easy to go through life with blinders on, oblivious to (and far too busy for) the joyful surprises waiting to be discovered at any given moment. If you want these little gifts of joy in your life, therefore, you may actually have to train yourself to notice them.

※

KEEP A GLOW BOOK

I suppose I really expanded my ability to notice little delights during the year when I was courting my wife, Nanette. Young, in love, and separated by hundred of miles, we were always on the lookout for innovative ways to keep our relationship close. One of our most successful strategies was the use of our "glow books" — little notepads we each carried with us constantly.

Throughout each day we would record good things we saw and experienced — small blessings, unexpected encounters, funny moments. I would receive an especially interesting assignment in my job as a movie artist, and I would write it down. My neighbor in the apartment next door would bring over a sample of her homemade stew, and I'd make note of that delicious offering in the book. Nanette would write of a dream she had the night before, a conversation with a classmate, a person she was able to help in her nursing position.

At night we shared our jottings in marathon phone conversations — creating burgeoning phone bills but also nurturing our growing relationship. (Even today, after many years of marriage, we share the joyful surprises of our days, notes in hand, during our nightly quiet time together.)

But my glow book turned out to have another benefit as well: It turned me into a more joyful person. During this phase of my life, I was somewhat impoverished and chronically overworked. I lived in a big, smoggy city far from the people I loved, and I had yet to have any success at selling my paintings. I had every reason to be discouraged or even unhappy. But as I jotted experiences in my glow book, I noticed I was becoming more and more aware of the beauty and wonder all around me. I was conditioning myself to look for joyful surprises.

Keeping a glow book or a joy-journal is something I would highly recommend if you find yourself a little rusty at recognizing the joy-gifts that come your way. You don't have to share it with someone else. The very experience of recording the miscellaneous "blesslets" you encounter in the course of a day—from the gold shaft of morning sun to the softness of your blanket at night—will build your receptivity and awareness. Once you begin looking, you may be surprised to discover just how much joy your world has to offer.

BE A BLESSING

If we are fortunate, we learn this strategy as children basking in the joy of our mother's smile as we present her with the gift of a lovingly plucked dandelion or a crumpled crayon portrait. We learn it as teenagers participating in service projects, as adults involved in church and community programs. We learn firsthand the joy-potential in serving others, and we color our own hearts joyful with every blessing we give out.

If these were lessons we didn't learn early, or if pain and disappointment has caused us to forget, we can still begin to add to the joy in our lives through little acts of serving. Think of it as giving perks to someone else as well as to yourself.

Here as in other areas of joy, small efforts can bring large cumulative rewards. Try holding your temper when the cashier makes a mistake and say something pleasant as you wait. Hold the door open an extra few seconds for a slow-moving person behind you. Read to a child. Send a check to a homeless shelter or volunteer to ladle soup.

It's all been said many times before—sow what you want to reap, do unto others as you would have them do to you—but it remains eternally true. We humans are set up in such a way that giving joy to others actually adds dabs of joy-color to our own hearts.

Developing a servant's heart, in fact, is such an important ingredient of joy that I want to discuss it more fully in an entire chapter of its own. For now, though, it's enough to recognize that your heart will grow steadily and dependably joyful as you make a point of sharing the joy by blessing others.

PURSUE YOUR PASSION — OR PUT PASSION INTO YOUR PURSUIT

If we are involved in doing what we were put on earth to do, a joyful heart is almost guaranteed — even in the midst of deepest difficulties. Consistent and durable joy is generated when we pursue a passion that is strong enough to carry us past pain, something so meaningful and absorbing that we can ignore unhappy circumstances.

I consider myself deeply fortunate to have discovered such a passion in my art. My work gives me deep pleasure and satisfaction; it provides me with a dependable joy-base. So does my family, the other joy-giving passion God has blessed me with. Like any family, we have our moments of difficulty and conflict. But loving each of them, being with them, building them up — these things are the collective source of my deepest joy.

Passion and joy, in other words, are intimately connected. If you find that durable joy is fading in your heart, you might do well to pay attention to your passions, your purposes, and your pursuits. Do you feel called to follow a direction that is not currently the focus of your life? If so, perhaps it's time to begin mapping out a strategy that enables you to pursue your calling.

At the same time, don't assume you can't be happy unless you're doing what you love most for a living. If that were true, only a tiny portion of the world's population would be eligible for joy! The truth is that deep, abiding joy is available to anyone who learns the secret of pursuing *every* task with energy and dedication, as though it were a calling.

In other words, if you are having trouble pursuing your passion, you can still find real happiness by putting passion into your current pursuits. Each of us can find our calling where we are, right now, if we only begin to see the higher purpose to our task. If your days are spent polishing floors, think of the lives that benefit from the cleanliness and order you are providing. If you teach children, focus on the generations of future families who will feel the impact of your efforts. The farmer provides nourishment, the builder gives shelter, the office worker offers assistance and solves problems for customers and fellow workers. The list is endless. Each of us, in our own way, has a high and unique calling on our lives, if our ears can only be opened to hear it.

The Book of Ecclesiastes advises us, "Whatever your hand finds to do, do it with your might."

Writer Carolyn Huffman (and countless posters I've seen) puts it another way: "Bloom where you are."

Wherever it comes from, it's still sound counsel. Approach every day of your life with dedication, as though you were an ambassador of a better world, and even the most mundane tasks can be transformed into inspiring sources of joy.

SAY NO TO THE NIBBLERS

You know what nibblers are. Nibblers are the nagging little worries and frustrations that eat away at your happiness and steal your joy. They are the insecurities that pull down your spirits, the fears that grab at your confidence, the guilts and gottas that replace your enjoyment of life with an unnerving tension.

Not long ago I woke suddenly early one morning and found myself wrestling with a whole school of life-draining little nibblers. "What if the new business deal doesn't go through?" "I should spend more time with my kids." "I really blew it yesterday!" The little voices attacked when my defenses were down and were making serious inroads on my joy by the time I woke up enough to fight them.

But how *do* you fight the insidious little marauders? Nine times out of ten, I've found, you can do it by telling the truth!

That's because nibblers are really liars. They like to plague us with problems that aren't really problems, situations we've already taken care of, circumstances we can't do anything about. So I have found the best way to counter their fibs and prevarications is simply to call their bluff.

That's exactly what I did when the nibblers attacked that morning. I addressed them one by one and told them no:

"No, that's not a problem because my well-being doesn't depend on deals going through."

"No, that's not a problem because I make a point of spending as much time with my kids as possible."

"No, that's not a problem because I've already admitted I was wrong and done what I could to correct it."

Occasionally, of course, I will realize that a nibbler or a set of nibblers derives from a situation that really does require some action on my part. In cases like that, I can still answer them no by making a specific plan: "No, that's not going to be a problem because I'm going to do *this* to take care of it."

Saying no to the nibblers, in other words, is simply a matter of facing reality. The truth is that worrying about problems—as opposed to resolving them—will never do anything but drain your heart of its joyful color.

CULTIVATE MINDFUL ROUTINE

By nature, I'm not a man who relishes routine. I tend to prefer unscheduled adventure to tried-and-true dailiness. But I learned long ago that I *need* routine in my life—and that I have more freedom when my days can rely on a predictable rhythm.

I like to paint first thing in the morning, for instance. I usually take care of any necessary business in the afternoon. At lunchtime I take a break and enjoy a sandwich in the studio or at a nearby coffee shop. After lunch I read a chapter or two in an interesting book. At six, I make the one-minute commute from my studio to our house and seek out my girls for some family time. And unless something unforeseen happens, I do these things, joyfully, every day.

Such repeated and dependable activities anchor my days, providing a sense of stability. The planned flow of my schedule balances my life, checking my tendency to go overboard with either work or play. And a reliable routine frees me to be more creative because I don't have to decide what I should do next.

But I'm not talking about mindless routine. I'm not talking about doing things just because I've always done them or because someone else thinks my day should go a certain way. That's a rut, not a routine, and ruts are rarely joyful.

Though each of us has obligations and needful tasks we'd rather not do, a joy-giving routine is a *mindful* routine — one that is deliberately chosen, fully embraced (even the dull parts!), and always flexible, subject to alteration.

I'm talking about taking deliberate charge of the various parts of one's day. For example, I remember clearly the jolt of joy I received when I realized I didn't have to follow the typical "exercise in the morning" routine. Eager to keep in shape, I had resolved to start every day with a vigorous run around our neighborhood. But then I would wake in the morning with my creative jets firing. Even as I laced my jogging shoes, I was dying to get in the studio and paint. Not surprisingly, my exercise commitment soon began to slip. I would skip a day, then another, until I was skipping more days than I jogged.

Then the revelation came. Instead of plodding on with a routine that wasn't working or throwing my routine out the window, I decided to make my routine fit my life. Now I go to work first thing in the morning. Then, after an hour or two at the easel, I stretch my muscles, lace up my shoes, and begin my neighborhood jog. The exercise and the change of scenery gives me the zest I need for the rest of my day — and the dependable rhythm of mindful routine adds another coat of joy to my already shining heart.

> *Joy is a mystery because it can happen anywhere, anytime,*
> *even under the most unpromising circumstances,*
> *even in the midst of suffering, with tears in its eyes.*
> — FREDERICK BUECHNER

LOOK FOR THE BIG PICTURE

Sometimes joy seems hard to come by, no matter how we've worked to build a durable heart-source of happiness. When disappointment and fear and confusion descend, it can be hard to discern the color of joy in our lives. That's when it helps to step back and look for the big picture, the traceable pattern in the tangle of events and emotions, and the blessing that often wears the disguise of suffering.

This lesson pressed itself most powerfully upon me in the early years of my marriage, when my wife began looking for a job in her field of nursing. Funds were tight. I was just beginning to sell my paintings, and we desperately needed her income as well as mine. But the only job available to her at the time was an all-night shift that lasted from seven o'clock at night until seven the next morning. Because we are both morning people and outdoor enthusiasts, the prospect of Nanette's being employed in this manner sounded dreary indeed.

Somehow, though, God gave us the grace to step back and see the possibilities in what looked like a sentence of gloom. We reminded ourselves that this would only be a temporary situation, and we made the conscious decision to treat it as an adventure by becoming temporarily nocturnal.

I shifted my schedule to match Nanette's, and I soon found I was able to work with great energy and concentration during those quiet evening hours. We slept days, with the help of earplugs and window blinds, and we spent

Nanette's "days off," which were really nights off, by exploring the world of nighttime—enjoying moonlit bike rides, shopping at the all-night supermarket, and generally observing a great city at rest.

Because we chose to look at the big picture, this potentially unpleasant phase of our lives turned out to be an enjoyable one. As a bonus, now that we have returned to daytime living, Nanette and I find more joy in mornings than we ever did before.

I try to remember that lesson now whenever unexpected challenges seem to dull my sense of inner joy. I tell myself that even the phases of my life that were different than I would have chosen have turned out to be blessings in disguise, so I can realistically expect to find something good in any current difficulties as well. In the end, maintaining that kind of big-picture perspective will help keep the joy-color of my life from being extinguished by externals.

THE LIFE OF THINGS

Behind the big picture of our life is another, unseen, picture. This is not life in its perceivable detail, but life in its flowing wonder, shimmering with iridescent beauty, pulsing with an inner will, constantly renewing itself with goodness despite the surface imperfections. This is life—as mysterious as a free-floating vapor that shrouds the hillsides, as solid as the earth beneath us.

Surely this is exactly the kind of life-affirming joy view that William Wordsworth meant when he wrote, in his famous "Lines Composed a Few Miles Above Tintern Abbey,"

> . . . With an eye made quiet by the power
> Of harmony, and the deep power of joy,
> We see into the life of things.

Seeing, if only in brief glimpses, this powerful and mysterious life force causes the color of your heart to be more than a passive characteristic. The yellow chair's appearance might be altered by changing light, but the paint will have its say as well. A yellow chair in sun or shadow looks different than a blue one would. The landscape around the chair looks different, too, for the golden hue influences its surroundings. And the color of a joy-filled heart has even more power than the yellow of a chair, for joy in a life is a source of light unto itself.

The color within us, in other words, can color the world around us. When my attitude shines with durable joy, the world around me also seems to glow golden.

Even in the shadows, I can discern the gleam of goodness and possibility. Even in the dark, I know I can always find my way.

My life shines with God's radiant blessings
when my heart is the color of joy.

LIGHTPOSTS
FOR LIVING

TWO

※

GETTING LITTLE

LIVING IN A PLAYFUL LIGHT

All grown-ups were once children —
although few of them remember it.
—ANTOINE DE SAINT-EXUPÉRY

※

"Daddy, look at me!"

My three-year-old daughter perched proudly atop our big cushioned armchair, her wiry little body poised for another stunt in our "family gymnastics" session. I turned my head just in time to see her turn a perfect somersault from the chair down to the pile of cushions I had placed on the living room floor. Bouncing to her feet like an Olympic gymnast, she treated me with a triumphant smile.

"Boy," I said, "that looks like fun!"

"It is, Daddy!" she enthused. "You do it, too!"

I shook my head, mindful both of the furniture and my not-quite-as-young-as-it-was body. "Better not, honey," I told her. "I'm sort of big for that chair, don't you think?"

She patted me on the shoulder before clambering up for another try.

"It's all right, Daddy," she said encouragingly. "When you get little, you can do it."

I laughed. It was just one of those adorable things that children say. And then, ping! — it hit me. In one of those flashes of insight that often emerge from conversations with little ones, I realized my three-year-old had neatly summarized a vital principle of living in the light.

"When you get little," she said, "you can do it."

She was right.

I thought of the inspiring story from the Bible, often quoted, in which Jesus admonished his followers, "Unless you . . . become as little children, you will by no means enter the kingdom of heaven." The same reality has been observed and restated by poets and prophets over the centuries. There are some important things about light-filled living that children know but most adults have forgotten.

It's as if, in our determined scramble toward adulthood, we leave some valuable treasures behind us. We would all lead better and brighter lives if, at least now and then, we made a point of "getting little" enough to recover them.

GROWING BIG AND LITTLE

I don't want to overromanticize childhood or to suggest that being child-like is an infallible route to happiness. Children, after all, are human beings, which means they are not perfect. They live in an imperfect world, which means they are not always happy. And they are also immature humans, which means that both their imperfections and their pain tend to loom large, untempered by experience or perspective.

Anyone who has ever tried to reason with an obstinate toddler or to comfort a heartbroken five-year-old knows that childhood is not a romantic idyll. And Peter Pan aside, never growing up is not a desirable option for anyone.

Besides, as every child instinctively knows, children are *supposed* to grow up. Little children long to "get big," and rightly so. Gaining experience and perspective and power, learning patience and discipline and self-sacrifice — all these things can enrich our lives and make us stronger, more settled people.

But how much better will our lives be if we manage to acquire the virtues and advantages of maturity without sacrificing the childlike qualities that keep us nearer to joy?

How much fuller and richer and happier will we be if we can manage to "get big" in wisdom and experience but still remain "little" when it comes to the joy-skills of curiosity, trust, honesty, and an enthusiastic savoring of experience?

I suspect, in fact, that many of the qualities we tag as "adult" aren't really a necessary part of maturity at all. They are simply the result of letting ourselves grow tired, bored, burned out, and overly careful—letting disappointment and fear and resentment and pride clog the arteries of our spirits. Instead of continuing to grow and move as the lifeblood of joy runs through our veins, we let our hearts wither and harden. I've seen it happen. So have you.

What's the cure—or better yet, the prevention—for such an attitude-sclerosis?

That's where "getting little" comes in. Even as we attempt to grow in perspective and wisdom and compassion, we can also make the choice to value and retain the wide-eyed spark of childhood that is ever ready to light a new fire of enthusiasm within our often-weary hearts.

No matter how old we grow, we always have the option of getting little enough to be joyful.

SPEND TIME WITH CHILDREN

How do we keep in touch with these priceless childlike qualities?

By far the most effective way I've found to keep in touch with my own childlike spirit is simply to spend time with little people.

I learn so much from my own four children as I talk with them, read to them, change their diapers, get down on the floor and share their toys, and even, at times, become frustrated with them. Even as I teach them how to walk, how to play checkers, how to ride a bicycle, they are reminding me how to laugh and jump and act silly, how to *really* look at a caterpillar, how to trust that my needs will be taken care of. The time we spend together almost always turns into an unforgettable course in remedial joy.

On the basis of this experience I wholeheartedly offer this prescription for remaining a child at heart: Have children. If this is not your desire or option, at least arrange to spend time with children on a regular basis. Treat your nieces and nephews to an afternoon at an amusement park, gather the grandkids for a sleepover, visit a nearby playground and soak in the youthful antics, even host a birthday party for the kid next door. Better yet, volunteer at your local public school, youth center, or hospital children's center. You'll find that even "borrowed" children will give you a great excuse to slurp a Popsicle, create a snow angel, finger paint, or just plain act silly.

If you haven't been around children in a while, you might need to be patient with yourself at first. Shifting into a child's rhythm can be a jolt for

someone accustomed to adult speeds—you may find yourself either lagging behind a turbo-charged toddler or trying to hurry a dawdler along. Your mind may wander while playing Candyland, and your spirit may rebel at having to read *Curious George* "again" after you've already read it fifteen times.

Making the shift is worth the effort, though. And the good news is— you don't even need to know what you're doing. Most children, I've found, are more than eager to welcome grown-ups into their world and show them the ropes of being a kid. The more you allow yourself to participate in their games, their stories, and their activities, the more of their childlike attitude— and their intrinsic joy—you will absorb.

REMEMBER THE HAPPY PARTS
OF YOUR CHILDHOOD

While you're spending time with little people, I also think it's helpful to try to reconnect with the happy child you used to be. Explore your memories and try to uncover those times that seem to glow in your mind—times when you felt carefree and joyful and in love with the world.

When I do that, I tend to remember swinging out over a big swimming hole and dropping down into the cool, dark water . . . or riding bikes with my brother . . . or sketching for hours under a big tree in the field behind my house. Although I have had my share of childhood pain and disappointment, these moments of joy seem to loom largest in my memory if I allow them to.

As you think back on your childhood, you might find yourself reliving warm summer evenings with fireflies blinking on the lawn, or big family parties when the relatives ate together and talked and laughed, or lazy afternoons when you curled up in your treehouse with your best friend or a great book.

Whatever your memories, the very act of recalling them can help you reconnect with the joyful, trusting, wondering child who still lives somewhere inside you. Try to remember how you felt, why you felt that way. Write down your happy memories just as you record the things that currently bring you joy.

It may well be, of course, that you cannot remember being a happy child. The bulk of your childhood memories may be so painful that you prefer not to remember them at all. Even then, you might be surprised at how powerful even a single happy childhood memory can be—perhaps a summer away from home or a special, loyal friend. But even if you cannot dredge up a single joyful memory from your childhood store, you can find ways of reconnecting to the joyful childhood you *wish* you'd had and of creating new memories for other children.

Speaker and writer Emilie Barnes did just this when she began holding annual tea parties for her granddaughter, Christine. This classic little-girl activity was something she had longed for as a child growing up with an alcoholic father and a mother who had to work constantly to support the family. Little Emilie's time was spent caring for the house and cooking the meals. She never had a tea party with her friends.

When granddaughter Christine was born, though, the tea parties began in earnest. Every year on Christine's birthday they worked together to prepare goodies, make tea, and decorate the table. Every year they dressed up and sat down to enjoy tea together. As years went by, other little girls came to join the fun. In giving her granddaughter the annual gift of a birthday tea—and now there have been more than fourteen of them—Emilie was also giving *herself* a tea . . . and connecting to a childhood joy she'd never experienced.

Backward, turn backward, O Time, in our flight,
Make me a child again just for tonight!
—ELIZABETH AKERS ALLEN

GET SERIOUS ABOUT BEING PLAYFUL

"What is your job?" I asked my seven-year-old one day.

Her answer was immediate: "Being a kid."

And she was right. Being a kid is exactly what a seven-year-old is supposed to be doing in her life. And what kids do, first and foremost, is play.

Children are masters of meaningful recreation. Instinctively they understand the purpose of play. They don't feel the need to separate work from leisure, "meaningful" activities from "frivolous" ones. They play because that's the way they learn. They play to practice new skills and to let off steam and to reconnect with joy. They play because it's fun. And they don't defend their playfulness. They *know* that playing is what they are supposed to do.

I am absolutely convinced that's true of us, too. We were never meant to lose our playful spirit as we reach adulthood. Neither are we to divide our world rigidly into "serious" work and "relaxing" leisure. The lines are *supposed* to cross. We live far more joyfully when we allow ourselves a playful spirit even in our work and when we inject meaning and purpose into our play.

We have a singing dentist in our hometown. He's notorious for his happy spirit on the job; he even sings as he walks down the hall for a consultation. This man gets excited by the craft of dentistry; he gets excited about constructing crowns and bridges. He thrives on the challenge of fixing teeth and the satisfaction of helping people. Being a dentist is fun for him.

That's the way I believe our lives were meant to be integrated—the child and the adult, the worker and the player. When our working selves are cut off from our playing selves—that's when our lives lose their childlike sense of fun and wonder. It's hard to live in the light when we let the tasks that occupy the largest portion of our day bring us nothing but boredom or frustration.

And yes, all this is easy for me to say because, like the singing dentist, I am extremely enthusiastic about my work. Painting is fun for me. I take my paints on vacation not because I'm a workaholic, but because painting truly brings me joy. And yet over the years I have also been able to find "an element of fun" (to quote Mary Poppins) in almost any task I've been asked to do, whether it was inherently pleasant or not. Most of the time, it was that element of fun that kept me going at the task.

When I was a cashier at an all-night gas station, for instance, I made up stories in my head about the many odd-looking patrons who stopped by (I sketched them during slow periods!). When I delivered pizza during my art-student days, I made a game of trying to beat my own record delivery time. When I painted backdrop after repetitive backdrop for a sign company, I joked with my fellow workers and experimented with new painting techniques. Even now, I love to enliven marathon print-signing sessions with vintage music or an old movie on the VCR. Working playfully helps me hold on to a childlike joyful spirit in the midst of what could otherwise feel like a grinding workload.

I've also had to learn over the years to master the flip side of the work-play equation: taking my play time seriously. Contrary to what many of us secretly believe, it's not "cheating" to take a vacation or a day off or even just lie in the sun on Saturday instead of mowing the lawn. When we participate in recreation we are doing just what the name implies: allowing ourselves to be re-created and restored. We have no more need to apologize for our play-time than my seven-year-old does.

At some level, at least some of the time, it's *still* our job to be a kid—and we'll have a lot more joy in our life when we recognize that fact.

☀

DO KID STUFF

When was the last time you climbed a tree? If you want to live a joy-filled life, that's a good place to start.

Once in a while, in other words, try making a point of actually playing the way you did as a child. Go to the park, climb in a swing, and try to touch the limb of a nearby tree with your toes. Pull out your son's skateboard and enjoy the way the technology has improved since you rode one of your own. (My recent attempt at this ended in a few minor scrapes, especially to my pride, but I had a lot of fun!) Challenge your daughter to a game of driveway basketball. Jump rope. Hop over (or in the middle of) a few rain puddles.

Physical play, especially, has a way of connecting you with the child you were. The very act of moving your body—creaky as it may be—can stir up memories of being young and joyful and fully involved.

But quiet play, too, can bring the child in you to the surface. I once saw an executive in the business-class section of an airplane pull a large coloring book from his briefcase and set to work. "My hobby," he told me as I shot him a questioning glance. Try it! Buy a box of crayons—splurge on the super-duper box of sixty-four colors—and spend an hour coloring. Or perhaps you'd like to work a jigsaw puzzle (one of the simple ones that even kids can do).

I especially recommend reading children's books—an old favorite, or something that catches your eye in the library. (My favorites are L. Frank Baum's Oz series and older versions of the Hardy Boy mysteries.) The best children's books have always been written for adults as well—and the advantage to reading them to yourself is that you won't have to read each one fifteen times!

For an extra-special dose of childhood, try giving yourself a day off from "school." Remember lazy summer days of sipping lemonade and skipping stones or just sitting, being bored? Remember snow days when an entire morning and afternoon of fun suddenly spread out in front of you as clean as the snow in your front yard? Re-creating that feeling for even a short time can nurture the childlike spirit inside your heart. Why not set aside a Saturday—a hot, hazy summer day or a nose-nipping winter one—for just such lazy-day pursuits? Just for eight hours, pretend you don't have anything to do but lie on the grass and watch the clouds. Gaze out the window and scuff your feet. Do a somersault on the grass, break out your favorite kite, sit on the porch and whistle . . . then wait for the joy to follow.

FOLLOW YOUR CURIOSITY

Curiosity is the basic state of a young child's mind. Little people have an intense curiosity about the world around them, an immense hunger to learn and grow, and a wide-eyed wonder about what they observe.

I've found that my life is always more joyful when I nurture that wide-eyed spirit in myself.

Curiosity and wonder come naturally to all human beings, but these wonderful attitudes are easily stilled by the pressure of schedules and responsibilities

and to-do lists. Something small and wonderful and mysterious may catch our eye, but we just don't have time to investigate. We may wonder why something is the way it is, but we're too proud and grown-up to ask, and we don't have time to do the research. A mysterious path may beckon to us, but we just don't have time to follow it.

The way to counter this child-stifling tendency, of course, is to make a point, at least sometimes, of following where your curiosity leads you. Once in a while, tag along behind the fire trucks and watch the fire instead of continuing on your way. If you've wondered where a certain road leads, take a turn and find out. If you find yourself wondering "why" about something, go to the library or call a librarian and ferret out an answer.

Most important of all, make time in your life for wonder. If at all possible, when something beautiful strikes your eye, stop and gaze at it. If you notice something unusual, let your eyes grow big. Ask questions about what you notice. You might even add the word *wow!* to your carefully cultivated vocabulary.

One interesting technique I've found for renewing my childlike curiosity and wonder is to deliberately change my perspective on the world. Children don't look at life the way adults do. This is partly because they lack experience, but I think it's also because the world *looks* different to them. They are closer to the ground, closer to details that may escape an adult's interest. And because they must physically look up to the majority of the world, it's harder for them to develop a superior attitude.

To gain a fresh perspective on your world, try actually looking at life through a child's eyes. Get down on the floor and look up at a world that is bigger than you, often out of focus, composed mainly of feet and knees and belt loops. Try looking at the bottom of your coffee table, the crawl space under your cabinets. (For the moment, resist the urge to clamber to your feet and find the broom!)

Then, just for fun, try to get up high as well. Climb a tree and perch in the branches—use a stepladder if you have to—or gaze down from the roof of your house. Find a hill and climb it and enjoy the vista from the top. Pretend you're king of the mountain. If the terrain permits, you can even drop to the ground and roll down the hillside with a chuckle or two.

After you've looked high and low, stand at your normal height and just gaze around at the world. Really look. Try to see your room, your house, your neighborhood, your town, as if you've never seen it before. Study the faces of people you love as if they weren't familiar. Take a route you've never tried.

The more you allow yourself to follow your curiosity and bask in your wonder, the more curious and wonderful the world around you will seem to grow.

STRETCH YOUR TRUST MUSCLES

By the time we reach adulthood, disappointment can make us suspicious, overly cautious, overcontrolled. We're not inclined to leave anything to chance. We fear our own mistakes because they make us vulnerable. We blame others because we fear being in the wrong. We insulate, inoculate, insure—do whatever we can to guarantee that things will be all right.

But the truth is, these efforts don't really work. No matter how hard we try, we can't guarantee that something bad won't happen, that we won't be let down, that we will never fail. We can't guarantee that all our worrying and arranging will produce good things, either.

All we can guarantee is that, if we spend too much of our energy trying to run the universe, we won't have much energy left for living joyfully.

That's why we need the priceless childhood treasure of trust—not foolish gullibility, but a comfortable willingness to let life work itself out without our continual tinkering and second-guessing and hedging our bets.

We forget that we too are children whose hearts must be opened,
trusting and needful of God's deep embrace
where all joy, all suffering is felt and borne.
—WENDY M. WRIGHT

Most children I know are comfortable with not always being right, not always knowing everything, not always having the last say, not always having to foresee every possibility. Right or wrong, they assume someone else is in charge of things, that their needs will be provided for, that their mistakes will be forgiven, that they will have another chance. As a result, they are freed to respond to the life around them—to work and play and look and learn with joyful abandon.

Where can we find that kind of trust as adults?

We can start by realizing that we're not nearly as big and competent and invincible as we think we are. Our shoulders just aren't big enough to carry the weight of the world—and yet somehow it keeps spinning. Maybe that should tell us something.

We also need to realize that trust, like joy, is an attitude we can choose. It's a habit of thinking—and one that is worth cultivating if we want to recapture a childlike optimism and expectancy in our lives.

We can choose to trust that things will work out. (Chances are, they will, and assuming they won't serves only to rob us of energy and motivation.)

We can choose to trust that even if events don't turn out the way we want, we will still have options and new possibilities.

We can choose to trust, at very least, that we just don't know enough to assume the worst.

It does help to believe, as I do, in a loving and benevolent God—or, at the very least, a divinely ordered universe. But even if you can't muster belief of this sort, you can still choose to trust in the richness and beauty of life, in the comforts of nature and relationships, in the dependable seasons of nature and even life itself. With effort, you can arrive at the conclusion that trust makes at least as much sense as distrust.

In the meantime, while you're working on your philosophy of trust, you can begin doing some things that help you live more openly and comfortably and trustingly. What kinds of activities and experiences help you feel safe and cherished and cared for? What kinds of encounters help you think the best of others? Making room and time for those kinds of experiences will also help you nurture your sense of childlike trust.

Daily rituals, for instance—from morning stretches to afternoon tea to bedtime prayers—can bolster your underlying sense that everything is going to be all right. So can cultivating the company of caring and trustworthy people—and working to be trustworthy yourself, for we tend to suspect others of our own faults and failings. Even simple comforts—from the warmth of a woolly afghan to the reassuring glow of a night-light in the hall—can reinforce your sense that all is well.

But oddly enough, one of the most dependable ways I have found to build my sense of trust is to take some risks. After all, as I learned as a boy, you'll never know whether the rope will hold unless you take hold of it and swing out over the water! In the same way, you'll never know if life can be trusted until you take the risk of really living.

Yes, it makes sense to be careful. Yes, it makes sense to look before you leap. But in my experience, at least, giving way to doubt and hesitation and fearfulness simply breeds more doubt and hesitation and fearfulness.

The times in my life when I have gathered my courage and launched myself into a new venture or a new relationship or a new idea with the trusting exuberance of a child leaping into Mommy's or Daddy's arms—those have been the times when I've discovered (even when my plans have failed) just how trustworthy life can be.

LET'S DO IT NOW!

When I think back to my own childhood days, the words that seem to fill my memories and epitomize my childhood are: "Let's do it!"

My brother and I would be sitting on our porch when one or the other of us would say, "Let's go swimming." Or "Let's go ride bikes" or "Let's go see what the kid down the street is doing."

And then the other of us would say, "All right! Let's go."

And we did. Unless Mom said no (and, I'll admit, sometimes even when she did say it) we did it right away.

I'm convinced there's something in that "let's do it now" mentality that is a vital secret to childlike joy. There's something inherently joyous about being able to think of something great to do and then jump into the idea with both bare feet.

So why don't we do it more often?

Because we're grown-ups, of course. Because we have schedules and responsibilities. Because we don't have time to be spontaneous.

But I think there's another, more serious, reason that we find ourselves unable to answer a "let's do it" with a "let's do it now."

The reason is that we're so busy cleaning up after yesterday and taking care of tomorrow that we don't even *notice* the now.

This is hardly a new observation, but it's a vital one. For although we can plan for the future and remember the past, the only place in time where we can really live is today, in the moment. This is where most children live most of the time. They haven't had enough past to develop preconceived notions about the future. Their focus is on what is happening at present and on what they can do with it. The current opportunity has their full attention.

That's an ability we all need to develop if we want to discover a childlike joy. We need to practice looking at the opportunities of the moment and saying "Let's do it now!"

I'm convinced there's room in most people's lives for a lot more spontaneity than we allow ourselves. Yes, our schedules are important. Planning is important and fun, even for children. (Our kids love to be involved in mapping out our activities, especially in planning campsites for our famous family road trips.) Routine is vital. Responsibilities should be tended to. Gratification must be delayed.

But not always!

If we want to recover a childlike joy, we need to understand that schedules and routines were made to serve us, not to rule us. (With proper discipline, our schedules can even be used to clear room for more spontaneity — but that's a later chapter.) Responsibilities were meant to nurture relationships and build our communities, not to prevent us from enjoying them. Delaying gratification doesn't have to mean delaying *all* gratification *all* the time.

It's a simple fact: The opportunities of the moment often can't be deferred. We either say yes—now—or we are saying no. If we want to unwrap the gifts that life gives us, we need to be willing, at least occasionally, to accept the package and tear at the wrapping with gusto and abandon.

Not too long ago, on a Saturday afternoon, I heard that a storm was blowing in and expected to hit the coast not far from a friend's beach house where we were staying. Sensible people would be advised to stay indoors. But as I watched the beautiful thunderheads roll in and the trees begin to dance, I announced to the children, "Grab your umbrellas, kids. We're going for a walk."

In this case, the adult and child roles seemed actually reversed.

"Aw, Dad, do we have to?" was their response. "We might catch cold out there!"

But I had to do it. And what a thrill that walk turned out to be. The waves were ten, fifteen feet high, roaring, crowned with spray—magnificent. The winds were so strong we had to lean forward to remain standing. Thunder rolled. Rain poured. I was drenched but exhilarated, awed at the beauty and the power of God's creation, rejuvenated from the decision to say, "Yes, let's do it now." And even the kids had fun.

You can't always do it, of course. And you do have to be responsible even when you're being spontaneous. (We stayed far away from downed power lines, and we went inside when the lightning started.)

But you really ought to do it when you can. If you want to nurture the child's heart within you, you need to practice saying, "Let's do it"—and then do what life is calling you to do.

Practice with little things first:

"Let's cuddle up and read a book—right this minute."

"Let's go take a walk around the block—now."

"Let's have a cookout at the park and invite the neighbors to go with us— tonight."

There will always be reasons why you can't, but you'll build a backlog of childlike joy within yourself if you do it whenever you can.

Jump in with both feet.

Tear the wrappers off the gift of life.

Do it now.

And then . . . why not try what I tried not too long ago, in our family room, during a certain family gymnastics sessions.

After my three-year-old turned another perfect somersault off that chair, I climbed up, perched myself unsteadily on the same piece of furniture, cast a wary eye on the stack of cushions before me.

Then I took the plunge. I rolled myself forward, managed to tuck my head beneath my shoulders, and landed more or less squarely on the cushions. The furniture was a bit worse for wear, but I was exhilarated.

My daughter was, too.

"You did it, Daddy," she squealed as I pushed to my feet. "I knew you could do it!"

We stood up together and smiled. Two children holding hands.

It's when I let myself get little
that I tumble head over heels into joy.

LIGHTPOSTS
FOR LIVING

THREE

A Picture of Harmony

Living in a Balanced Light

We have come . . .
To that still centre where the spinning world
Sleeps on its axis, to the heart of rest.
—Dorothy L. Sayers

It's a beautiful morning . . . calm, still, shrouded in mist.

The air is soft and warm, though a hint of a breeze stirs the leaf tips and ruffles the surface of the little stream at your feet. All around you are signs of life—birds chirping in the trees, a chipmunk scurrying through underbrush, a gentle splash as a frog hits the water—and yet a sense of expectancy hangs in the air as you gaze out toward the gleam on the far horizon.

Even as you watch, the seam between earth and sky brightens, and everything around you seems to shift its attention to the spot where low-hanging clouds evolve from purple to pink to orange and gold. You sense the gathering crescendo as the brightness builds.

Then, in one of those moments that will forever hang on the walls of your memory, the sun pushes its way over the horizon. For a second it seems to hang there, liquid gold, bathing the world with a wash of triumphant joy.

And suddenly you realize you've been holding your breath, awed into silence by the picture of dynamic harmony spread out around you.

Just for this one moment, it seems, everything is as it should be.

Just for the moment, all is truly right with the world.

THE BEAUTY OF BALANCE

Have you ever received the gift of a morning like that, one of those magic times that seem to epitomize the way that life should be? If you have, that's a moment to hold in your heart. Return to it often, for it has the power to inspire you with the kind of life you really want—a life that is full yet balanced, pulsing with vitality, yet smiling with peace. Even if you haven't been gifted with such a moment, the act of picturing it in your mind can still bring you a step closer to a sweeter, more satisfying existence, for it is the pictures we hold closest to our hearts that shape our lives most powerfully.

That's exactly why I paint the way I do. My goal is to try my best to create the kind of scenes that catch the heart and lift the spirit and fill the mind with visions of life as it *could* be. Every element in my paintings, from the patch of sun in the foreground to the mists on a distant horizon, is arranged in an effort to summon back those perfect moments that hang in our minds as pictures of harmony. My deepest desire is that my work will help people aspire to the life those kinds of images evoke.

Consider, then, what kind of everyday reality would evoke the same feelings of rightness and peace and harmony that a perfect sunrise instills—the same sense that everything is as it should be, that there is space and time enough for everything important. What combination of activities and involvement would paint a picture of harmony in your heart and mind and daily existence?

To me, the hallmark of such a harmonious life is balance.

Imagine a life where there is plenty of time, plenty of energy, plenty of opportunity for everything you feel is important—plus a little left over for some things you simply enjoy. Think about a life where work commands your energy and involvement but does not require you to sell your soul, where leisure time relaxes and restores you, where you enjoy both solitude and friendships. A life where physical activity, intellectual pursuits, emotional involvements, and spiritual devotion support each other instead of fighting for your attention. Who wouldn't want such a balanced, harmonious existence?

To me, the vision of that kind of life is especially compelling because balance has sometimes been a challenge for me. I have always been very dedicated to my work and at times a bit grandiose in my thinking. My natural tendency is to pour too much of myself into some things and not enough of myself into others. In the past, I have said yes to too many possibilities, too many peripheral pursuits, and ended up having to say no (or at least "later") by default to other things I truly value. I am deeply grateful to my wife, my daughters, and my colleagues for hanging in there with me while I was learning a few things about balance.

The good news, though, is that I *am* learning. Over the past few years, in fact, I have learned more than I ever knew about the kinds of choices that lead to a balanced life. Nanette and I often remark these days on what a difference these balancing lessons have made in our life together, how learning to balance has brought us more peace and satisfaction.

COMPOSING A LIFE

How have I learned to keep my balance in the midst of a family life and career that at times seem to grow more demanding by the day? The starting point for me was realizing that balancing a life is not all that different from balancing the compositional elements in a painting. The very choices that contribute to creating a picture of harmony on a canvas can help me move closer to harmony in my daily life.

And though it's common to think of balance in terms of "getting organized," at this point I am not talking about the challenge of whipping all life's details into shape. I'm referring more to the big-picture decisions that set the stage for the little ones. This chapter, in other words, is about the basic principles of balance and harmony that provide a frame of reference for all the rest.

When I begin the initial process of blocking in a canvas, I am making decisions about what goes where, what colors and tones will dominate, what elements will be most important. And similar decisions, too, form the stable foundation for a balanced, harmonious life. As I think about composing my life, I must begin by making some foundational decisions about how I'll spend my time, where I'll invest my energy, and why I'm doing it all in the first place.

The more I think of it, in fact, the more I've come to believe that the decisions that shape a balanced life are not that different from the decisions that create a painting full of harmony and peace. For if I've done what I set out to do in a painting, a few things will be true about it.

First, as I've said, the composition in the painting will be balanced. That is, the "building blocks" that combine to create the picture—from flowers and trees to house and bridges (not to mention lightposts!)—will be arranged in a way that moves the eye along rather than letting it wander aimlessly over the painting or hover distractedly over a single area.

If the balance is right, there will be a general sense that everything is in its proper place. The overall effect, however, will be of rhythmic movement, balanced give-and-take—I like to call it dynamic equilibrium—rather than stiff, geometric formality. Instead of balancing a large rock on the right with a large rock on the left (a kind of balance that would be visually dead), I might offset a large but indistinct stand of trees on the left with a tiny but visually arresting figure of a deer on the right.

But compositional balance is not the only aspect of a painting that imparts a sense of peace and "rightness." If an artist does the job well, the relationships of color and tone and light and shade within the painting will also seem harmonious. All these elements will work together in a way that seems natural and inevitable and lovely rather than jarring and discordant. If you have ever seen a painting where one brushstroke of bright color seems to jump out and dominate the composition, you know what I mean: Unharmonized color can be disturbing to the eyes. When everything is in harmony, though, the whole painting will seem to sing.

If I want my life to resemble a harmonious sunrise scene, then, rather than a snapshot of a cluttered alleyway, I need to decide which activities are meaningful and important to me and invest the most significant aspects of my time and energy in these. I'm not just talking about my work and responsibilities here. Just as important to my balanced life are adequate rest, healthful nutrition, regular exercise, and leisure activities that refresh and renew me. These, too, must find their rightful place in my schedule and my priorities.

Most important, I need a basis for judging when to leave one activity and start another. When have I worked long enough and need a break, and when do I need to push a little harder? I need a way to determine when an activity I enjoy can be worked in with all my other responsibilities and when it just doesn't fit with the direction my life is going.

The key to answering these questions and making these determinations is the same in life as it is in painting: I need to establish the focal point or center of interest.

WHERE'S THE CENTER?

The focal point on the canvas is the most important part of the entire composition. It may not be in the physical center of the canvas; the most interesting paintings, in fact, often have centers of interest that are discernibly off center. But still, this spot on the canvas is unmistakably its visual and emotional center, the point where the eye lights first and where it eventually comes to rest again. Each rock, tree, or house, every brushstroke or choice of color, finds its rightful place in relationship to that vital focus.

Have you ever browsed through one of those *Where's Waldo?* books? Each page of these books is a visual puzzle—a cartoon scene crammed with people, animals, buildings, and hundreds of miscellaneous objects. Everywhere you look there is activity: children playing and eating ice cream, delivery trucks maneuvering through packed streets, people working and playing and just standing around talking. The detail is amazing and entertaining. And somewhere within each composed page is Waldo, a tall, thin, smiling man sporting a red-and-white stocking cap. The entire point of the puzzle is to locate this fellow somewhere amid the busy throng.

Well, it's fun, but it isn't easy. Sometimes finding Waldo can be downright frustrating. Your eyes roam to and fro in that cartoon crowd, seeking in vain for the man in the striped hat. And for me, at least, looking too long at one of those crowded cartoon pages is simply exhausting. Because there is no discernible focal point (Waldo is *supposed* to blend with the crowd and not draw attention), their total effect is of jittery, nervous energy, not of harmonious peace.

That's precisely why a distinct focal point is important to a peaceful life as well as a peaceful work of art.

A center provides a starting point from which to choose all your other involvements, a reference point by which to judge what will balance and what will harmonize. It provides a kind of resting place where you can return at the end of a day and renew your sense of how your life fits together.

In a sense, then, the focal point is the organizing principle that determines all the other organizing principles in your life.

It's not exactly the same thing as a goal or a priority, as important as these things are. A focal point is broader than a goal, more compelling than a priority, more fundamental than either.

Simply put, the focal point in your life is the commitment or involvement that provides its deepest meaning, commands your deepest loyalty. It is the fundamental value that determines your goals and priorities in the first place, the starting and ending point for decisions large and small.

Here's a personal example. Because I am a very busy, somewhat ambitious man, I tend to be goal-oriented and fairly strict about maintaining priorities. At this point in my life, all my goals revolve around two basic ones: my family and my work. But underlying *both* of these commitments is an even more fundamental center, the focal point that has led me to choose these priorities.

For me, that fundamental focus is my deep desire to use my gifts, my talents, my time and resources in ways that have meaning and significance beyond my own years on earth, ways that will benefit the world after I have gone.

This focus is a direct outgrowth of my faith both in God and humanity, my foundational sense that life has a meaning and that individuals can truly make an impact on the future. I believe that every one of my blessings, be it my family, my material possessions, whatever talent I possess—in short, everything I have or am—has been given to me for a reason, an eternal

purpose. And I have come to believe that I can best achieve that purpose by attempting to create uplifting works of art that will stand the test of time and by trying to raise strong, loving, secure children who can have a positive influence on future generations. Thus, my fundamental focus flows naturally into the priorities of my life.

Now, if this sounds a bit grandiose, let me assure you I don't spend long hours every day contemplating the eternal implication of every decision, any more than a person gazing at a painting will stare for hours at the focal point and ignore the rest of the painting. The focal point in my life is simply my understanding about what is important in life and my sense of the overall reason I've been put on this earth in the first place. For me, keeping it clearly in view—or at least in my peripheral vision—is crucial to making the decisions that keep my life balanced.

Not everyone, of course, will have the same focus that I do. Some might even question whether a clear central focus is really necessary to a painting or a life. Can't we simply paint what we see and let the picture arrange itself? Can't we have multiple centers of interest . . . or just take life as it comes along?

The simple answer to that question, of course, is yes.

It's possible to paint—and to make it through life—without a balanced center. Many painters and many human beings do just that.

Certainly there are competent painters who simply fill a canvas without regard to focus (though these canvases often end up with a focus the artist never intended). Certainly there are philosophers who hold that life has no actual "center," that we must simply make up our own meaning as we go along. And quite certainly there are people who live long, reasonably successful lives without ever stopping to question what the focus of their life is. Others organize their lives around a focus that is inherently trivial or false or even evil. (You don't need to be a ruthless tyrant to center your life around a drive for money or power.)

But remember that we're talking not just about a successful life, but about a balanced one. We're talking about what it takes to organize your existence into an inspiring picture of peace and harmony. And to achieve that sense of harmonious rightness, I truly believe the center needs to be a true and inspiring one. Whatever your personal faith or belief system may be, at some point in your journey through this life you must stop to ask yourself, "Why am I here?" Your process of answering this most foundational of questions is a vital first step toward living a life that is a picture of balance, harmony, and peace.

> *To gain a new perspective, our questions must be simple and profound.*
> *What is important? Who is important?*
> *What are we going to do about it?*
> —DON OSGOOD

FINDING YOUR FOCUS

Some people are blessed from a young age with a clear sense of what their center is. These are the people who seem to be born with a mission, who rarely entertain doubts about what their purpose in life is.

These people, I believe, are rare.

For the majority of us, the center of interest develops slowly, over time. Sometimes it seems to swim gradually into view, like a photo in a bath of darkroom chemicals. Sometimes it shifts position as we make conscious and unconscious decisions about what really holds meaning for us. Often it remains elusive, shrouded in mystery, even as it shapes our thoughts and our beliefs and our goals and our actions.

This is true of the focus in my paintings, too. Sometimes I know what it will be from the moment I conceive of the work. Sometimes I discover it as I go along. The focal point of a different work may be brilliant and clear . . . or it may be only subtly emphasized.

All this is to say that you shouldn't worry if the focal point or the center of interest in your life is not yet clear to you. At the same time, I believe you will benefit from devoting a little time to finding your focus.

Note that I didn't say "set your focus," in the sense that you would set a goal. In order for a life-focus to *be* a life-focus, it must come from within, from that deep part of you that knows what's important even when your conscious mind just isn't sure. It's not really something you decide; it's something you discover.

This means, of course, that there are no "shoulds" in finding your focus. Your focus will not be the same as mine. It will emerge naturally out of your sense of who you are and why you are here, and it will most likely resonate with your God-given talents and interests. Your focus is, I believe, a kind of spiritual vocation, a sense of what you are *called* to do.

I recently heard of a woman in Colorado who is known in her area as "the bird woman." She is the one to call if you find a fledgling fallen from a nest or a hawk with a broken wing, because she has learned the skills of caring for birds, rehabilitating them, then releasing them in the wild. What began for her as a simple interest in birds has become a full-time vocation. She long ago shelved her plans to travel in her retirement because her birds require her full attention. And though the constancy of their need can be a problem at times, she thrives on a life that is balanced around this central passion. "It would be a shame," she told the interviewers, "to miss the thing you were put on this earth to do."

That's exactly the kind of purpose to look for, to pray for, to wait for expectantly, even if it takes a while to emerge. If you can begin to evolve a sense of what you were put on earth to do, all your other decisions will begin to fall into place.

A STATEMENT OF PURPOSE

In my experience, at least, careful *listening* is the irreplaceable key to finding your purpose. If your purpose is going to emerge from inside you, you need to pay some attention to the wants and needs of your heart and soul and spirit. Times of prayer and simple meditation—daily or weekly or even monthly—will nurture the spiritual connection that I believe is absolutely vital in evolving a focus that is truly personal and intrinsic to your life.

Most specifically, I think you will find it helpful to "listen to your life," as writer Frederick Buechner puts it. Learn to look back on where you've been and what you've done, both recently and in the distant past, in search of what is truly important to you. Note the thoughts and experiences that loom large in your memory, that seem to have special meaning and significance. For example, have you always been a "people person," or do you, like me, enjoy working alone? Do you thrive on a busy city pace, or does relaxed country living bring out the best in you? Do you feel especially satisfied when you are working with your hands? Do you love to daydream and imagine? Analyzing your life in terms such as these may well be helpful in discovering your proper focus.

I know of a woman, for instance, who recently realized that the most fulfilling times in her life were the times when she was listening to friends and helping them with their problems. This realization has helped her see that her life-focus should include using her listening skills and her understanding of human nature to make a difference in other people's lives. As a result of this recent sharpening of her focus, she is considering going back to school to become a professional counselor or a social worker.

I also think it's helpful to look forward, to imagine what your thoughts and feelings might be as you approach the end of your days. What will be important to you then? What will you regret or be proud of? What will you treasure? What would you want your obituary to say about your life and its meaning? Thinking forward to tomorrow can help tremendously in determining your focus for today.

I'm the only person my age I know, for example, who regularly fantasizes about having grandchildren. I derive great joy from imagining the days when I will be an old man surrounded by my family. But realizing how much I look forward to those days has also helped me clarify my focus by showing me how deeply I care about contributing to future generations.

Over a period of time, from exercises in listening such as these, a center of purpose and meaning will begin to emerge, clear and unmistakable or shimmering in its shroud of mystery. You might not see it all at once clearly. It may come slowly, in a series of smaller revelations. However it appears I think you'll find it helpful, as I have, to verbalize your understanding of your focus in the form of a written life purpose or mission statement.

Organizations write mission statements all the time, of course, as a way of establishing unity and purpose. They use them as a basis for decisions and growth, and also to make necessary course corrections as they develop over time. A mission statement, in essence, is a brief description of the company's purposes and reason for being. While it is descriptive, it's also prescriptive, a statement of "why we are here" and "what we want our corporate life to be about." In that sense, it's a summary of the company's focus.

Writing a mission statement for your life can be just as useful. Sit down with a sheet of paper and try to capture, in about ten words, what you feel is the primary focus of your life. Try to capture what is important to you, what you believe the purpose of your life is, what you were born to do. Don't write what you think your focus *should* be. But don't be afraid to put down a focus that still feels unrealized in your life—something you feel your focus *might* be.

If you find this difficult, try writing in the past tense, pretending you are writing your own, most satisfying memoir. Or use one of these lead-ins to get you started: "I am here on this earth to . . ." "My purpose in life is . . . " "The most important thing in my life is . . . "

Here are some examples of possible life-mission statements for a variety of circumstances:

"I am here on this earth to teach children the skills they need to be successful in the world and to help them awaken to the joys of the written word."

"My purpose in life is to protect my family and to give them a sense of safety and security."

"The most important thing in my life is to learn about love by cultivating an intimate, meaningful relationship with another human being."

Don't let this exercise intimidate you. The very act of setting these things down is a learning exercise, not a commitment to unchangeable destiny. Write in pencil, if you like, to remind yourself that you are not deciding, but seeking to *discover*, your focus. Once you've articulated it, revisit your mission statement periodically to see if it holds up. Revise and refine it if you need to. Work with it until it feels just right.

Once that focus begins to take shape, the decisions you make about balancing your life will be a lot easier.

֎

BALANCING YOUR ACT

Locating the focal point or center of interest is a vital part of my planning for a painting, but it's far from my *only* consideration.

In fact, if I tried to create a painting with *only* a focal point, I'd end up with nothing more than a red dot on white canvas. To even consider a focal point or center of interest as an end in itself is ludicrous. The focal point has meaning only in relation to the other elements in the composition.

The kind of painting I create is comprised of buildings and trees and clouds and mountains and people and animals, all of which must find their proper place and position on the canvas. The life you lead is similarly full of tasks and relationships and thoughts and events. Every day of your life, you must make decisions about the placement and importance of all these things.

Think for a minute of the disparate and sometimes contradictory elements you balance in your life on a daily basis: preparing meals, getting to work, helping children with homework, meeting deadlines, connecting with friends, reading the newspaper, doing laundry, fixing the car, relaxing with a movie. Every day you face the challenge of deciding how much time and energy you should devote to your job, to your family, to urgent tasks, to big-picture planning, and to interesting possibilities you wish could be part of your life. Every day you decide when to say yes, when to say no, when to say now, when to say later, when to say definitely, and when to say maybe.

So how, once you have defined your focal point, can you make those kinds of balancing decisions? I have found that several basic strategies are helpful.

BLOCK OUT YOUR CANVAS

First, it helps me to "block out" space on the canvas of my life to take care of priority items. This process is similar to what I do when I first begin sketching in the major compositional areas of a painting. Working first with pencil and charcoal and then with flat washes of paint, I mark off the areas on the canvas where I will place the most important elements.

When I was working on the early stages of a painting called *Garden of Prayer*, for instance, I sketched in a simple neoclassical gazebo just to the right of center. This little structure would eventually emerge as the center of interest for the painting. Then, to the right and the left, I marked in two strong vertical paths of light—a garden path on the right that would emerge into an area of golden sunshine directly beside the gazebo, and a cool stream on the left that would reflect a band of cooler, misty light. Between these two swaths of light, to shape them into graceful curves and create a shaded back-drop for the gazebo, I marked off stands of trees and curving stream banks.

At the end of this process I had a picture that resembled a scene viewed

through textured glass—the details and the nuances were missing, but the basic forms were in place. I could then add rocks and flowers and tree trunks and even a tiny, mysterious figure behind a garden gate without fear of disturbing the basic visual balance of the painting.

I find it's just as helpful to organize my life by blocking out space for what is most important to me, assigning each element a place in the landscape of my daily flow of time and energy. On the broadest level, I reserve weekdays for work and evenings and weekends for family. From that basic division, I block out general areas for smaller priorities. There's a spot in the early afternoon for exercise. Business meetings take place either early on Monday mornings or on weekday afternoons. Saturdays are for chores, errands, and an occasional outing with the kids. Sundays I set aside for church, playing together, or relaxing as a family. Nighttime, after the kids are in bed, is usually reserved for Nanette. Assuming we can find a sitter, we also try to block off an evening every couple of weeks or so for a date.

Once these general parameters are in place, I try my best to stick with them, to give each the attention it deserves. When I am painting, I turn off the phone, discourage visitors, and throw my energy into the work at hand. When I am in a meeting or brainstorming with colleagues, I try to keep concerns about my painting from my mind. And when I am at home with the kids or alone with Nanette, I try hard to give them my full attention instead of stewing over a painting challenge or a business dilemma.

Sometimes I even imagine the various important activities in my life as fitting into separate boxes with lids that can be opened and shut at the appropriate times. I see my daily and weekly schedule as a matter of going from box to box, opening each one in turn, enjoying or working with the contents, then closing the lid and moving to the next box.

Thus, when I go to the studio, I'm opening the work box. When I leave the studio and shut the door, I put the lid on the box and trust that the contents will keep until another day. When I turn the doorknob and enter my home, I am lifting the lid of the family-time box. When I leave for my daily exercise, I close the lid on work time and open the important box that contains fresh air, physical exertion, and as often as possible, the companionship of my wife.

In addition to the mental exercise of opening and closing the boxes, I also use physical cues to help me separate the different areas of my life. Because

I tend to be a visually motivated person, I have found that this helps tremendously in my effort to honor the areas I have blocked off. Though my studio is right next to my house, for example, it is still a physically separate space. My commute to work is short (I just walk next door), but the act of striding down the walk and opening the studio door symbolizes that I'm going to work. In a smaller way, the act of standing up from my big wooden easel, walking out the door, and relaxing into one of the big lawn chairs in our garden symbolizes that it is time for a break. Driving into the city for a meeting or even turning on the speakerphone for a conference call tells my body and my spirit that it's time to do something else.

In reality, of course, the contents of my daily "boxes" do—and should—overlap. Nanette and I do sometimes spend our husband-wife time discussing business or the kids or even settling a sibling dispute. (Sometimes our talk during daily exercise time will be the only communication we'll manage all day long.) The kids do come visit me at the studio. Often, assuming that everyone is behaving, I'll set up a little easel and let them work away on their own projects. And obviously, since our business is integrally connected to my work as an artist, I can't keep the two entirely separate.

My life is my life, in other words, and it's lived as a whole, not in a series of separate categories. I'm sure that's true for you, too. Nevertheless, I think you'll find that blocking off space for the important concerns of your life will do wonders for your sense of peace and harmony, because it will assure you that each "box" will be routinely tended to.

You probably can have it all. Just not all at the same time.
—ANNA QUINDLEN

LIMIT YOUR PALETTE

Another helpful strategy I keep working on, one that is also analogous to a painting process, has to do with choosing the basic range of "colors" in my life. By "colors" I mean the general kinds of experience and activity that will help my life revolve harmoniously around its focal point. I have found that limiting myself during a given period of time to a certain range of interests and experiences can do a lot toward keeping my life peaceful and harmonious.

In painting, I have found that I achieve a more unified, harmonious effect if I limit the "palette" of a painting—its general range of colors and tones. Although I love color, all colors, if I were to squeeze out a dab from every tube in my studio for a single painting, the result would be noisy and chaotic rather than peaceful and harmonious. Similarly, if I were to indulge in all my interests and follow all my fascinations, I would find it next to impossible to lead a balanced life.

Growing up in a very limited small town probably fueled my ongoing hunger for experience—all kinds of experience. I love the high, the lofty, the inspiring, but I also harbor a fascination for the seamier underside of existence. I love both gardens and junkyards. I crave a settled family life, but there's also a part of me that wants to be a hobo. I *was* a hobo once, for an entire summer during college, and I have never forgotten the sense of fun and freedom I felt then.

At this particular time of my life, though, certain things are objectively true: I am the father of four small children. I am part of a reasonably large, publicly owned corporation. I create paintings and write books about a simpler, more tranquil way of life. I am also a man whose personal Christian faith causes him to care about his influence on others. And all these things are central to the way I am, or at least the way I want to be—to the things I want my life to count for.

So what do I do with my fantasies of donning a worn leather jacket and heading for the sunset aboard a souped-up motorcycle? For the sake of harmony in my life, I have chosen to limit those impulses to an occasional road trip with Nanette. Because I have chosen to limit my palette to a certain range of colors appropriate to this time in my life, the vast majority of my actions and my involvements are more in keeping with my role as a family man, a professional artist, and a person with business responsibilities.

But I want to stress that this is not a matter of refraining from "questionable" activities because of a need to maintain a certain image. I simply find great joy in sparing myself the inner conflict of being pulled between too many widely divergent pursuits. Even though some types of experiences may tempt me at times, I have learned that the sense of peaceful appropriateness my chosen limits bring me is infinitely worth the temporary loss of a couple of "colors" in my life.

Besides, even within the limited "palette" I've chosen, I've discovered an entire spectrum of possibilities for fun and meaning. These days, for example, the majority of my leisure time is spent in activities that can be done with the children. But rather than let myself feel confined or limited, I have tried make the most of the long list of enjoyable things I can do with my kids.

Our family has camped together, hiked together, and visited endless theme parks together, sometimes with babies crying in the background. We have sailed on river rafts with little ones in backpacks, and on one occasion we all climbed aboard a stunt plane. We have played every board game imaginable and have often packed our easels and tramped into the woods to paint. (This activity usually lasts about fifteen minutes before one or more of the kids is ready for a new challenge.)

The point is that the limitations of any given phase in life, when embraced in the interest of harmony, can offer a fulfilling set of possibilities. Are you single? You have certain freedoms and unique opportunities that you simply would not have if your life were different. Are you married? The same is true for you. Are you a single parent? Married with children? Retired with no children in the home? The trick, as I see it, is to look at each set of circumstances as liberating rather than confining, a unique and compelling palette for the work of art that is your life right now.

REMEMBER TO KEEP MOVING

Have you ever tried to balance yourself on one foot? If you hold yourself completely still, you can't do it! You must keep making subtle shifts and corrections just to stay upright.

That's true of keeping your balance in life as well. If you want to maintain a balanced, harmonious existence, you have to keep moving—at least a little bit.

Or here's a better example: A seesaw on a playground is in essence a board balanced on a base or fulcrum, and the fun of playing on it lies in moving up and down, changing your position while remaining in a kind of dynamic equilibrium. You could make the whole thing more stable, perhaps, by putting the board on the ground, but the result would be both boring and meaningless. It certainly wouldn't be balanced.

Life—even a balanced, harmonious life—was never meant to be static and unchanging. Choosing a focus and balancing our life around it is a life-long process of choosing, adjusting, changing. Sometimes you tilt one way, sometimes you tilt another. At times you invest extra time and energy into one aspect of your life, then later you correct the balance by an emphasis on another aspect of your life. (A tilt is not really an imbalance unless it never tilts back.)

This very changing, tilting dynamic, I've found, can sometimes fool us into thinking we're losing our balance when we're actually doing all right. Sometimes we have to remind ourselves to relax a little more, to worry a little less, to trust the way we've blocked in the composition and set ourselves up for balance, to remember the big picture and not let the details overwhelm it.

If the center is in place, if we've paid a little attention to making balancing and harmonious choices, if we're not afraid to move, to change, then all we really need to do next is enjoy the ride.

Up, down, with a constantly changing perspective on the canvas of your life—it's the way things should be. A dynamic equilibrium—full of richness and balance and harmony and joy.

When I find my focus and keep my balance —
I find that all is right with my world.

LIGHTPOSTS

FOR LIVING

FOUR

LIGHTPOST 4

業

THE ABUNDANCE
OF ENOUGH

LIVING IN THE LIGHT OF SIMPLICITY

Our life is frittered away by detail.
An honest man has hardly need to count more than his ten fingers,
or in extreme cases he may add his ten toes, and lump the rest.
Simplicity, simplicity, simplicity!
—HENRY DAVID THOREAU

業

Ah, the simple life!

Who doesn't long for it, especially these days when life seems to get busier and more complex by the hour? In a culture that is summed up and symbolized by the superhighway—both asphalt and information!—who doesn't yearn (at least part of the time) to find an exit to a simpler way of life?

Think about it the next time you're trapped in bumper-to-bumper traffic or weaving through the crowd at the mall. Think about it while you're juggling (not balancing!) a thousand things that need to be done. Couldn't you go for a lazy afternoon on a front porch, sipping lemonade and talking with friends? Couldn't you appreciate a quieter, more purposeful schedule—get up, pursue your workday, come home to a few chores, have dinner and relax with family or friends, retire for a restful sleep?

A lot of people feel that way, apparently. There seems to be a national craving for simplicity, a movement toward old-fashioned modes of living. My first book, *Simpler Times,* examined in detail my own philosophy of living a less complex life. And, many of the collectors who buy my paintings and my books say they are drawn to them because they depict times and places where daily life really did seem simpler—not easier, perhaps, but a little slower, a little quieter, a little less complicated. Some have told me that my paintings, especially the ones of quaint English cottages or stately Victorian houses, speak to their yearnings for an era when life moved at an easier pace, when there was time and emotional energy for savoring every day.

SHOPPING FOR SIMPLICITY?

I share those yearnings, too. Why else would I paint those images of horse-drawn carriages and big front porches? I applaud the urge and the effort that leads people to read about simplicity and buy paintings that inspire them with simplicity. I believe that catching the vision for simplicity is the vital prerequisite for exiting the fast lane and changing life for the better.

At the same time, I can't help wondering if many people are vicariously experiencing simplicity through books and paintings without ever realizing it really is possible to enjoy the benefits of simplicity in their daily lives.

As far as I can see, for all the talk about simplicity, very few of us live lives that can be described as simple. In fact, most people that I know repeatedly make one or two basic choices that keep their lives out of control and leave them feeling chronically rushed and dissatisfied. And with the constant onslaught of such destructive busyness, there is simply no room for the glow of joy to begin growing in our lives.

Simplicity, you see, must be more than simply a yearning. It must be more than nostalgic pipe dreams, more than living in the past or pining for the "good old days." Simplicity, like joy, must involve a choice—or actually, a series of choices. Just as you can choose joy, you can choose simplicity as a guiding light in your life. You *can* choose to step back from the frenzied rush and enjoy a better, simpler, more light-filled existence. Believe it or not, it really is possible to slow life down and enjoy each moment. You really can have control over the sheer volume of activities and involvements that seem to drain your energy and motivation.

But simplicity doesn't come automatically. Not anymore. (Maybe it never did.) If you want a simpler life, you have to learn to make simplifying choices—choices that involve words like *no* and *not now*. You have to learn the simple art of *enough is enough*.

But here's the surprise. Learning to say no to what you don't need really begins with learning to say yes to what you have.

True simplicity, in other words, begins when you learn to enjoy the amazing abundance of what is already yours.

THE CHALLENGE OF FREEDOM

Simplicity is different from focus, different from balance, different from harmony—although simplifying your days can make the process of focusing and balancing much easier. The process of simplifying your life is primarily the process of making room, clearing out space, and letting some light into the cluttered closets of your days. In a sense, the act of simplifying your life is really the process of giving yourself freedom—freeing mind and schedule from the overload of activities and occupations that inevitably weigh you down.

Unfortunately, simplicity doesn't always *feel* like freedom—at least not at first. In fact, although the simple life may sound irresistible, the actual practice of simplifying your life can feel threatening. Simplifying means saying no, giving things up, passing choices by. It can feel like losing something important. And I believe there are some important reasons for this.

In the first place, saying no goes against our basic human territorial urge to acquire, get more, conquer, stock up. The fear of not having enough and of losing what we already have can be so deeply ingrained that we feel pain at eliminating anything from our lives—even when we know we have too much to handle. So choosing simplicity is in part a matter of reminding yourself that the peace of mind you gain from simplifying your life is worth the natural twinge of anxiety that comes with letting go of the extra possessions and activities that complicate your life.

More important, I believe, the move in the direction of simplicity goes against the dominant voices of our highly materialistic society. Despite our recent cultural infatuation with the simple, so much that goes on in our society contributes to keeping our lives complicated, complex, too fast, too full.

No wonder the actual act of getting simple feels more like swimming against the tide. You *are* swimming against the tide—but toward the shore of serenity.

Your first and most important simplifying choice, therefore, may be simply to understand why simplifying your life doesn't always seem so simple. This means learning to recognize some of the cultural messages that trick us all into complicated thinking. We hear these messages so often—from our friends, from the media, even from our families—that they quickly come to sound like truths. I know they sometimes sound that way to me! But the more I manage to adjust my thinking and realize that complexity is not the normal state of affairs for living, the simpler and more satisfying my life becomes.

THE MYTH OF MORE IS BETTER

The first cultural message that works against simplicity is what I call the Myth of More Is Better. It involves the basic assumption that, in order to be happy and satisfied, we constantly need to acquire more, take on more, become involved with more and more.

Mostly, the "more" we need is interpreted in material terms. Often without even realizing what we're doing, we buy into the assumption that we must constantly build our material base, acquiring ever more valuable or up-to-date possessions. Our whole culture is built on the drive to "trade up" everything from vehicles to houses to computers to jobs in order to lead a more worthwhile life.

The most obvious expression of the "more is better" fallacy is our shopping culture. Have you ever stopped to think how much of your energy is taken up with hunting for new stuff, purchasing new stuff, bringing new stuff home, finding a place for it, then storing or getting rid of the old stuff to make room for the new stuff?

In our culture, shopping is a primary form of entertainment. It is also the basis of a consumer culture deliberately aimed at keeping us on the prowl for more. We shop as something to do, we shop to ease our anxieties, we shop to replace the stuff we've thrown away or just grown tired of, we shop for bargains in order to feel virtuous. We chuckle at phrases like "When the going gets tough, the tough go shopping"—but we chuckle because we recognize the truth of such statements.

No wonder malls have replaced pubs and parks and even houses of worship as primary gathering places for a community. Shopping seems to be the common denominator—the complicating common denominator—of our cultural life. Sunday is no longer a day of rest and worship. It has become a day of driving from one crowded shopping experience to another.

But the Myth of More Is Better applies to our activities as well as our possessions. I often hear people complain about how busy they are, but their complaints tend to be colored with a tint of pride in that very busyness. At a very basic level, we tend to assume that the people with the most activities in their lives are the most important, the most valuable, the ones who deserve to be rewarded. We assume that about ourselves. No wonder we complicate our lives with so many competing activities.

An important corollary to the Myth of More Is Better is what I like to call the Myth of Gotta Have It. We are conditioned to think that the very existence of something new means we must have it in our lives. We "gotta have it" in order to be happy, successful, and fulfilled. Unfortunately, much of the time, we feel we "gotta have it" now, even if having it means going deeply into debt.

Technological advances, especially, seem to fuel the Myth of Gotta Have It. The very speed of technological change seems to trigger a fear of being left behind, of not being on the cutting edge. Surely there's something wrong about a culture that declares a cutting-edge computer chip "old" after a few months and "obsolete" after a few years. At the very least, adopting such a hyped-up way of thinking is guaranteed to complicate your life.

It's important to understand that it's possible to buy into these myths (often literally *buying* into them) without consciously believing in them. It is quite possible sincerely to believe that more is *not* better and yet be actively shopping on the premise that it is! The myths of More Is Better and Gotta Have It are so ingrained in our society that we don't even notice them—until, perhaps, we travel to a country that doesn't subscribe to them quite as religiously.

Living for an extended time in a country village in England was what woke me up to the pervasive power of these myths. Our refrigerator in England was small because food shopping was something we did every day, as a way of staying in touch with our neighbors as well as with the greengrocer and the town baker. There were no subdivisions scattered for miles along the highway. Instead, homes clustered snugly around the village center, so people could bicycle or walk most places they needed to go. Possessions were cared for and handed down with pride rather than used negligently and discarded.

What I saw in that area of rural England was a snapshot of life in our country about fifty or sixty years ago. Somewhere along the line we've lost that kind of simplicity . . . and some of our joy along with it.

THE MYTH OF MY LIFE IS NOT MY OWN

The second misconception that I believe complicates our lives immeasurably is what I call the Myth of My Life Is Not My Own. I hear the echoes of this myth all around me, especially in the woeful litany of "I just don't have time."

Like you, I often hear people lamenting that their schedule is just too full for them to do the things they want to do in life. The assumption seems to be that their time—and by extension, their lives—is owned by other people, be it their boss, their family, their neighbors, their employees or customers. They live as though they were passive observers in the process of living—bondservants with only a small pittance of "free time" to spend as they choose.

I believe to the depth of my being that this common assumption is a lie, and a dangerous one at that. The truth is that by definition *all* our time is free time, ours to spend or invest as we choose. Our lives are a precious gift

presented to us at birth. We are responsible only to ourselves and to our Creator for what we do with this marvelous gift. Regardless of our circumstances, then, the simplicity or complication of our lives comes from our own choices, not from what the outside world imposes upon us. And regardless of the messages our culture gives us, we *can* choose simplicity—by choosing what we include or exclude from our lives.

Now, I am not advocating a formless life, devoid of consequences or obligations! We need other people. We need to earn a living. We need to eat and sleep and exercise. We need (I believe) a spiritual foundation and an ethical code in our lives. Because of these needs, a certain portion of our time and energy will of necessity be spent in the process of nurturing relationships, doing our jobs, caring for our bodies, feeding our souls, and doing what we believe we are called to do.

At the same time, I believe we will never lead a truly simple life until we realize that every one of us does "have time"—exactly twenty-four hours of it in every day. The days of our lives don't belong to any other person. There are no slaves in America today, thank God. And unless you are physically living in forced servitude, no one can decide how you spend your time but you.

Your days belong to you. Your hours belong to you. Each minute of every day is yours. You can choose to spend your minutes responsibly. You can spend them purposefully, on activities that have meaning for you. Or you can spend them—if you choose—on a multitude of extraneous involvements that complicate your life and steal your freedom.

Because I believe this, I find it absolutely amazing how easily human beings surrender their God-given hours and days to the pursuit of activities that they really don't care about and that don't come close to bringing them peace and serenity or satisfaction. Because of habit, because of outside pressure, sometimes just because it's easier, they simply engage in what crosses their path. If a neighbor keeps a spotless home, they feel compelled to slave daily at housework. If they're asked to serve on six committees, they climb on board. If all their friends are getting married, they start searching for a spouse. Because they don't have a bigger plan in mind, their activities are chosen for them. That's when they start feeling helpless, put-upon, overwhelmed by life's complications.

But don't misunderstand. I'm certainly not saying that we shouldn't do housework or serve on committees or get married. I'm simply talking about the common tendency to do whatever comes along instead of choosing activities that fit in with *your* goals and priorities.

For example, Nanette and I once had friends who tried hard to convince us that we should own a speedboat. "Just think of all the family togetherness!" they'd rave. "What better way could you find to build memories?"

But the more we examined the issue, the more we recognized that parking a powerboat in the garage and hauling it out every weekend just wasn't what we wanted to do. Our family tends to enjoy simpler, less mechanical pursuits, and I'm not the kind of guy who derives satisfaction from constantly tinkering with motors and gadgets. So we decided to say no to the idea of boat ownership.

For our friends, the boating lifestyle was a great asset to family life. For us, it wouldn't have been a good fit. Making these kinds of choices means knowing yourself and your family well enough to choose what would be meaningful and beneficial to you, regardless of the choices that might work well for others.

Here's another, slightly different example. An elderly friend of mine is retired. His time really is his own. And this particular person has many interests. He loves to fish. He loves to travel. He has always wanted to paint. And yet, for years after his retirement, he wasn't doing any of those things. Instead, he spent most of his time parked in front of the television. His health was suffering, and his spirits were low. I would ask, "Hey, why don't you grab a pole and go fishing." As the TV blared in the background, he would answer, "I just don't have time."

From my viewpoint, it was easy to see where this person's time—and his life—was going. From his viewpoint (shaped perhaps by a bit of apathy but also from sheer habit), there were no more windows left in his life, no space for true enjoyment. And while his life was not complex in the sense of being crammed with activities, it was still clouded over by the Myth of My Life Is Not My Own.

This story, fortunately, has a happy ending. Over time, as this particular gentleman adjusted to retirement, he decided to take up painting. (I admit to having some influence here.) Now he's hooked on an activity that truly contributes to his happiness. His days revolve around a core of this creative activity. He and his wife are traveling more—and he takes his easel along. They go to the river and fish, but he also pulls out his paints while he's there. Because he managed to challenge the myth that his life was not his own, he was able to move toward an infinitely more joyful life.

Here is a simple revelation that is bringing me a lot of freedom:
There is enough time. . . . I am discovering that I have
exactly the right number of hours and minutes
and seconds to accomplish and do everything that I need to do in my lifetime.
— CLAIRE CLONINGER

THE MYTH OF AUSTERITY

Here's yet another misconception that I think prevents some people from simplifying their lives. They tend to think of simplicity only in terms of extreme examples, and they simply can't see themselves going to such extremes. They may envision Henry David Thoreau living alone in the woods or an Amish family making do without cars or zippers. And since they can't picture themselves doing either, they simply shrug and turn their cars toward the expressway one more time.

Although I have deep respect for both Thoreau and the Amish, I don't

think that kind of radical simplicity is necessary or even desirable for every-one. Each person's needs and calling are different, but I don't believe the majority of us are called to abandon our homes and our jobs just to discover a simpler, saner existence.

I, at any rate, haven't abandoned any of these things. My family enjoys more material blessings than I would ever have dreamed of as a boy: a house, a studio, two comfortable family-sized vehicles, nice bicycles for everyone to ride, and even a touring motorcycle for weekend cruising. We maintain a busy schedule in close proximity to a fair-sized city. We do, on occasion, go shopping. And yet, increasingly, we find that our decisions are made on the basis of what makes our lives simpler, slower, and more fulfilling.

Though our life is full, it is far from frantic or harried. It revolves around a few basic priorities and responsibilities we have chosen, plus a number of simple pleasures. And whenever we feel that things are becoming too com-plicated, we don't hesitate to do whatever is necessary to simplify. If a pos-session has begun to demand too much maintenance or waste too much time, we get rid of it. If an activity or commitment has crowded our lives too much and is not related to our central focus, we do what we have to do to end that activity.

We are constantly in the process of weeding out the extraneous from our lives so that we will have time and space to focus on what is important to us. We just don't let a preconceived idea of simplicity dictate what those choices are.

For instance, a telephone headset allows me to carry out routine painting chores while taking care of phone calls. Call conferencing allows me to attend meetings without driving in to our company's business office. The fax machine cuts lag time out of correspondence. The answering machine frees me from the need to jump whenever the phone rings. Each of these inventions allows me to work more efficiently and builds more space into my day. Because they afford me more freedom to think or relax or be with my family, I welcome them into my home as simplifying agents.

Television, on the other hand, has proven to be such a time sponge that Nanette and I long ago banished it from our home. It's not that we think television is intrinsically bad. We have simply found that it tends to fill any unoccupied space in the hours of a day. To us, even the process of deciding what to watch and of limiting the hours we watch is more than we want to bother with; we much prefer to eliminate it altogether, to spend our family time talking and playing and interacting with one another instead of staring in unison at the tube.

Your family's situation, of course, is different from mine, and your simplifying decisions may not resemble mine or anyone else's. You may find, for example, that the answering machine is a complicating nuisance or that the television actually simplifies your days (though this I doubt!). Or you may find the automatic bread baker a simplifying godsend while another person finds it just another object to clean on the kitchen counter. Owning more than one vehicle might cut down on unnecessary errands for one family while actually adding to another family's total maintenance worries.

Simplicity, you see, isn't a one-size-fits-all state of being. It is more a direction than a destination, a value or a principle rather than a set of rules about what you should or shouldn't have. Any decision that can open up space in your life, allow more time for what you care about most, and help you feel more peaceful is a simplifying decision.

⚜

MOVING TOWARD SIMPLICITY

Challenging the myths of simplicity is just the beginning step toward simplifying your life. Next comes the actual clearing-out process. You need to decide what is helpful and what is extraneous, figure out when to say no and when to say yes, and learn to create some space in your schedule by weeding out activities and involvements that weigh you down and hurry you up without contributing to your peace and satisfaction.

How do you identify which activities are extraneous? The easiest way I know is to walk through a day in your mind. Imagine yourself getting out of bed, getting dressed, brushing your teeth. Picture the activities of a typical day, one by one. If you like, do this with your daybook or appointment calendar in hand. Where are the "knots" in your daily or weekly schedule, the spots that tend to make you feel frustrated, overwhelmed, or hurried? Do you tend to be stressed in the mornings or before dinnertime? Do weekend chores overwhelm you? Are you distressed by the stacks of to-do papers piling up on your desk? Those are the places to begin in your move toward simplicity.

One woman I know who tried this exercise realized that the clutter on her dining room table was a distinct roadblock to simplicity in her life. Because the table was a flat, empty surface that everyone passed on the way to their bedrooms, it tended to collect books, papers, mail, and other miscellaneous materials. Whenever dinnertime rolled around, she faced the chore of clearing off all the mess in order to set the table. Sometimes she found herself just pushing the papers aside or even serving meals on trays in the den.

Once she realized how the mess on the table was complicating her days, however, this woman was able to address it very simply: by resetting the table immediately after a meal had ended. After clearing the table from dinner, she brought out the breakfast dishes. After breakfast, she had the children set the table for lunch. She soon discovered that removing the temptation of that empty flat surface handily solved the problem of the cluttered table. As a bonus, setting the table ahead of time dramatically simplified the process of getting ready for the next meal.

※

SIMPLIFYING OPTIONS

Because you are trying to simplify your life, resist the urge to take on all your complications at one time. Instead, start with one item—one snag in the serenity of your days—and begin asking yourself some basic questions.

Say, for instance, that your lawn is beginning to look like a jungle or a desert (depending on your climate), and the tasks of mowing and trimming have come to seem like complicating chores. When you dedicate your weekends to taking care of the lawn, you seem to have no weekend left for play or rest. When you *don't* take care of it, the pain of watching your grass die and the weeds take over just adds to your stress level. Every time you think of your lawn, you can feel a little knot form in your stomach.

How do you simplify that situation? The way I see it, you have several options.

One possibility is to delegate the task to someone else. For instance, perhaps you can recruit one of your children to be in charge of the lawn. Perhaps your spouse would appreciate the exercise.

Another related possibility would be to pay for more freedom. This is a real option even if your funds are limited. Money spent in the interest of simplifying your life is usually money well spent—a far wiser option than spending it to buy more stuff. Even if you can't afford a gardener, perhaps you can hire a teenager or even one of your own children to take care of the lawn. Alternately, you could pay to install a sprinkler system or even have the lawn reseeded with low-maintenance native plants.

Yet another possibility—perhaps the most obvious—is to downsize your life to eliminate your problem. You could choose, for instance, to move to a condominium where all outdoor maintenance is taken care of or to a city apartment whose "lawn" is a windowbox.

If none of the these possibilities seem feasible, you have yet another option: You can choose to change your attitude about the activity and assign it a different role in your life. Rather than removing the problem, in other words, perhaps you can take steps to remove the emotional stress attached to it.

A friend of mine has adopted just this strategy with regard to his lawn. Although he can well afford to hire a gardener, he has decided that the process of caring for the yard can bring him enjoyment and bring his family closer together. So he has chosen to combine lawn care with family quality time. On any given evening, you can see this family out in the lawn mowing, watering, pulling weeds, planting flowers. They have started a butterfly garden, and everyone has great ideas for what they want to do in "their" yard. What once was a stressful complication to a busy family's life has been transformed into a time of simple and joyful togetherness.

These, then, are the important questions to ask regarding any aspect of life that stands in the way of simplicity:

Can I delegate it?

Can I pay to have it taken care of?

Can I downsize and eliminate it?

Can I change my attitude and assign it a different role in my life?

Chances are, the answers to these questions will be enough to move you steadily down the path of simple joy.

PLANNING FOR THE WINDOWS

Quite a few years ago, Nanette and I moved into a house that was built against a hill. We loved everything about that house except for the basement, which was really just the space behind the blank wall that held the house up

on the hillside. That basement area was musty, dark, and not even finished—the dirt of the hillside slanted right up across the floor. But we had a great idea—we would transform that dark, dirt-filled space into a bright, sun-filled master bedroom.

It's a good thing we didn't know what we were getting into! The whole process turned out to be more work than we ever imagined. First came the arduous task of hauling out all that dirt, transforming the sloping hillside into a vertical wall. Then we had to finish the walls, adding insulation and then drywall. Next, we had to plan for the windows in the outside wall, positioning them to bring in plenty of light without glare. We had to choose the right windows to install, the right window coverings, and we had to be careful to maintain the structural integrity of the building. Then came the process of actually cutting the holes in the walls and installing the windows.

When the windows were finally in—what a difference! The sunlight streamed into our future bedroom, transforming it. Even though the walls were not yet painted, the carpet not yet installed, the furniture not in place, that swath of sunshine made the whole difficult project seem worthwhile.

Even so, I couldn't help thinking how much better it would have been had the original contractor planned for those windows in the first place.

Watercolor artists do just that when they are first sketching out a new painting. In watercolor, the "highlights" of the painting are usually indicated by places where the white paper shows through, so the artist must know from the very beginning where *not* to put the paint. Often, in fact, a watercolorist will apply a frisket—a kind of liquid masking tape—to protect the areas that should be left white. After the painting is complete, the frisket can be removed to reveal the white highlights.

The frisket, like a window, is most effective when planned from the very beginning. And I find this is true about simplicity as well. It's never too late to make simplifying choices in your life. But my life seems much brighter when I "plan for the windows"—deliberately structuring my daily schedule with a little extra light and space in it. Even when my schedule is packed, I try to make sure that it has plenty of breaks, both large and small, and I try to resist the urge to fill in these empty spots with more activities.

This means that I guard my downtime jealously. I rarely work through lunch. I almost never miss my daily walk—although I often combine this with "couple time" for Nanette and me. At dinnertime, we don't answer the phone, and we ignore the doorbell.

Increasingly, as well, I am setting aside Sundays as a true Sabbath—a day of rest and relaxation that I guard from outside encroachments. I find that when I do this as a matter of policy—staying away from the studio, making use of the answering machine, restricting our family activity to simple walks, reading, games, or outdoor activities in addition to going to church—I am less tempted to sneak in errands, shopping, chores, and other items on my to-do list. As a result, I've begun to learn how to relax into the slower pace of a true day of rest. From there, in expanding circles, a sense of peace and simplicity extends to the rest of my life.

Whether or not you have a habit of weekly worship, the policy of setting aside some sort of Sabbath can pay enormous benefits in terms of cutting "windows" in your life. Even if you can't set aside an entire day every week as sacred to the cause of simplicity, try setting aside a single morning or evening, or perhaps a weekend once a month. Whatever period of time works for you, build it into your schedule like a window in the wall.

What is this Sabbath "window" for? Think of it as a little glimpse of retirement, a preview of the years ahead of you when entire weeks will be yours to spend as you like. Do you have a hobby you've always wanted to pursue? Do you want to study nature by exploring the outdoors? Do you never get enough time to read? This is your day, your window of opportunity. Spend it as you choose, but resist the urge to think of it as "empty" space where you can put more of your everyday activity. Think of it instead as filled with rest and renewal—and guard it tenderly, for simplicity's sake.

'Tis the gift to be simple, 'tis the gift to be free,
'Tis the gift to come down where we ought to be.
And when we find ourselves in the place just right,
'Twill be in the valley of love and delight.
—TRADITIONAL SHAKER HYMN

THE JOY OF FASTING

One of the most helpful "windows" I have found to build into my life is the practice of fasting. By fasting, I mean I set aside times in which I choose to depart from my normal meal patterns. In recent months, for instance, Nanette and I have set aside a twenty-four-hour period every week for a juice fast. From after dinner on Monday until dinner on Tuesday, we consume only juice and water.

Our purpose in doing this is partly spiritual, partly physical. We like the sense that we are giving our bodies a rest and a chance to cleanse themselves. We also appreciate the heightened spiritual awareness that seems to accompany this physical discipline.

But an unexpected benefit that we have derived from fasting is a renewed appreciation of simple foods. After a day of fasting, nothing tastes better than plain bread, raw vegetables, and fresh fruit. Fatty food seems by contrast heavy and almost intolerable. Our senses and our bodies get in tune with what our mind has known all along: simplest really is best.

What we have learned from fasting, in other words, is that sometimes the most effective way to say yes is to say no. When we learn to say no to the often frenzied cries of our wants and needs, we get a clear look at what is truly good and wonderful. Instead of dissatisfaction and hunger for more, we find ourselves experiencing more joy and contentment.

We have discovered so much simple pleasure as the result of our food fasts, in fact, that we have looked for other ways to enrich our lives through the discipline of fasting.

Some days we have gone on "technology fasts," unplugging appliances and enjoying life by candlelight. We have gone on spending fasts, challenging each other to ferret out fun activities that cost nothing at all—from a bike ride to a jigsaw puzzle from the shelf to an old-fashioned parlor game from an antique book I own.

With four small children in the house, we have not exactly managed to go on "talking fasts" (days of silence), but we see this as a future opportunity for enjoying simple silent communion. And we do try to set aside regular quiet times, short periods when we withdraw from the noise and distraction of daily interaction in order to pray and listen for God's voice in our lives.

Through all these times of fasting, large and small, we have found ourselves more and more enamored of simple living and more motivated to make that simplicity part of our everyday lives. Even after we turn the lights back on, plug the phone back in, switch on the radio, and sit down to dinner, our period of disciplined deprivation—of saying no—has whetted our appetite for simple pleasures. And when we partake of those pleasures, we find the taste intensified and all the sweeter.

SAYING YES AND SAYING NO

Jaded appetites, I've discovered, are the unavoidable consequence of our more, more, more culture. When every corner boasts a fast-food restaurant with children's menus and toys, when neon signs and movie marquees beckon along every block, it's easy to fall for the Myth of More Is Better. It's easy to buy into the fallacy of assuming that somebody else is running our lives, to fritter away our time to the point that we have no room left for simple joys. It's easy to reach the point where simplicity seems threatening and scary instead of liberating.

Whenever that happens—whenever you find you're caught in the traffic jams of a complex, confusing, overwhelming life—that's when it's time to pull into the exit lane of simplicity. That's when it's time to delegate, to hire, to downsize, to change, to reprioritize. That's when it's definitely time to build in more space, either temporarily or as a permanent part of your schedule.

Most of all, that's when it's time to cultivate the satisfying experiences that make simplicity worthwhile—the sights and sounds and thoughts you encounter only when you're not distracted by too much to do, too much to worry about, too much stuff in your life.

Think about it: What are the simple pleasures that have delighted you in

the past? What are the joys you've lost track of in the complexity of your current life? Think of a day of baking bread, a hike in the woods, an afternoon under a spreading oak tree. Think of harmonicas and pennywhistles, of visits to a park or a museum, of birdwatching in the afternoon or stargazing at night. Think of impromptu basketball games or involving embroidery projects. Think of watermelon warming in the sun and juicy peaches fresh from the tree.

When you do, you'll find yourself right back where you started—with the vision of just how wonderful the simple life can be. And I have discovered time and again in my own life that any real and lasting change begins with a vision. If you can envision the simpler life you crave, you can achieve it. As that image of the life you long for begins to emerge, simply plan the steps that will set you on the path toward it.

Say no to the Myth of More Is Better. Say no to the voice that tells you that you don't have time for the best things in life. Say no to the myth that simplicity has to follow a prescribed path. Say no to the things you know do nothing but complicate your life.

But first, say yes to a vision of simplicity. Proclaim, once and for all, that enough is not only enough, but enough is truly abundant!

This is the kind of simple life you've read about in books and sighed over in paintings. It's the kind of life you've dreamed about, longed for, sought out. And it really can be as wonderful as you've imagined it.

All you have to do is choose it . . . now.

It's a simple, liberating reality—
the best things in life are mine for the choosing.

LIGHTPOSTS
FOR LIVING

FIVE

FILTERED SUNSHINE

LIVING IN A POSITIVE LIGHT

Whatever things are true, whatever things are noble,
whatever things are just, whatever things are pure, whatever things are lovely,
whatever things are of good report,
if there is any virtue and if there is anything praiseworthy—meditate on these things.
—THE BOOK OF PHILIPPIANS

You've heard it said: "You are what you eat."

Given what we know about nutrition, that's probably true. It's also probably true that you are what you read, listen to, look at—even what you say and think. Unfortunately, with the cacophony of sights, sounds, ideas, and events that assault us daily, what many of us really are is stressed, anxious, and overwhelmed!

I'm talking about the messages that shout from your mailbox and your e-mail box, about the piles of newspaper in your recycling bin and the magazines that seem to cover every available horizontal surface in your home. I'm talking about the recorded music that follows you everywhere—in your car, in your office, at the mall, even piped into your ears by stereo headsets while you enjoy the great outdoors. I'm talking about television, the most pervasive messenger of all, which fills every corner of our lives, providing a constant white noise in the background of most homes and even intruding into such public spaces as restaurants, airports, and waiting rooms. (I keep hoping that restaurants will begin to offer non-TV rooms the way they currently offer non-smoking areas.) I'm also talking about the merchandise lining store aisles, billboards lining streets and highways, signs everywhere, hundreds of phone calls from solicitors eager to pitch their product . . . in short, messages, messages, and more messages bombarding us throughout every day of our lives.

No wonder we often end up feeling anxious and confused instead of peaceful and motivated. There's just too much to absorb in the first place. And much of what there is to see, hear, read, think about, and talk about just isn't conducive to joy.

So here's a radical notion—one that you may have some trouble accepting but that can pay enormous joy-dividends in your life: You don't have to let it all in. You don't have to look at everything, hear everything, read everything, any more than you have to eat everything on the menu.

Why is this a radical notion? Because we live in a society that glorifies the concepts of complete information and total disclosure. We place a premium on up-to-the-minute reporting and state-of-the-moment information, rarely stopping to question whether consuming all these facts really makes us wiser and more knowledgeable. As far as I can see, our compulsive openness to stimuli does nothing more than keep us stirred up and disoriented. It certainly doesn't seem to bring us any closer to ultimate truth.

Of course it's important to be honest. Of course it's important to be informed. Of course it's important to open ourselves to reality. We need outside input in our lives, just as we need sunshine to grow and be healthy.

But as this slightly reformed sun-lover is learning, what we really need is *filtered* sunshine.

PARASOLS OF PEACE

I learned early in my career as a painter that limited or filtered light is inherently more interesting and beautiful than direct sunlight. I learned that people are irresistibly drawn to depictions of dappled sun on a wooded path, morning light sifted through mist or clouds, lamplight piercing the gloom of dusk. Filtered light is soft and gentle. It feels safe and comforting rather than harsh or glaring. And it still does its job of brightening and illuminating the world.

The elegant ladies of past centuries understood some important things about filtering sunshine, too, that we are just now relearning in our sunblock era. I love those old paintings of Victorian women strolling in parks or gardens with their lovely fringed parasols and wide-brimmed hats. Those were elegant accessories, but their real purpose was protection. Victorian ladies believed that too much sunlight could be damaging to the skin. Medical research over the past few decades has shown that they were absolutely right.

I believe that is also true about the "sunshine" of information that bombards us every day of our lives. We need it to live, but too much of it or the wrong kinds of it can be bad for us. Filtering and limiting what comes into our lives and into our minds not only makes our existence more joyful; it can protect us from emotional and even physical harm.

And here's the important point. Filtered sunshine is no less real than the powerful, glaring sun of a cloudless August afternoon. It's simply sunshine that has been softened to a healthy level.

That's exactly the goal of filtering the input in your life. You don't have to deny reality or live as a hermit to spend your days under a parasol of peace. All you have to do is learn the fine art of choosing what you will allow into your life, mind and heart on a daily basis.

⚘

WHAT IS BENEFICIAL

The key to filtering is setting up and adhering to policies of deliberate selectivity. This involves making decisions ahead of time about what kinds of information have a positive influence on your life and developing strategies for keeping other stimuli at bay. This is a very specialized form of simplifying your life.

What filtering means to you personally depends on many factors: your age, your profession, your tolerance for "sunshine," your intellectual needs. The key is to make some basic decisions about the amount and the kinds of data you are going to allow into your life and then enforce those policies to the best of your ability.

I find that most of the filters I select for my life have to do either with the amount of information coming in or the kind of information I allow in.

Filtering the *amount* is crucial in these days of information overload, when even the most isolated of us seems to be pummeled with data. Advances in media access and the advent of the Internet seem to be exponentially increasing the amount of information available at any given time. In computers, I am told, one of the newest toys is "push" technology, in which an Internet service actually visits your computer and feeds it "up-to-the-minute" information. You don't have to retrieve the information. It simply comes to you at any hour of the day. And the fact that by the time you read this paragraph such technology may be commonplace or replaced by even more sophisticated technology simply underscores my point.

Too much information, too fast, is overwhelming. It's stressful. It eats at your joy, and I believe it can even be dangerous. Trying to process too much information is like living in an apartment so noisy that you can't hear the emergency sirens down the street. For self-preservation, you simply have to turn the volume down—and that means limiting the amount of data that you try to sort through on a daily basis.

I also recommend that you consider the *kind* of input you filter from your life. I don't just mean avoiding violent or upsetting material, though I certainly don't think any of us need to clutter our lives with that. But here I'm also talking about the trivial, the shallow, the negative, the distorted. Why distract your mind and spirit with words and thoughts and images and memories that don't help you achieve the kind of joyful life you want?

The apostle Paul once wrote, "All things are lawful for me, but not all things are beneficial." I believe that's very true of what I let myself see, hear, and experience. I find that certain kinds of broadcasting, music, programming, reading material, and even conversation are not beneficial to me in my quest to lead a peaceful, joyful, meaningful life.

Some things that I read (such as cynical or nihilistic literature) accustom me to negative habits of thinking. Some things I hear or watch (such as violent or bloody films) cause my adrenaline to begin pumping at stressful, unhealthy levels. Some kinds of friendships (with pushy, shallow people) feed my weaknesses and subtly push me toward pride, while others (with needy, whiny people) simply drain me of energy and motivation.

Who needs it? I prefer to surround myself with the kind of input that uplifts me, expands my mind, and settles my spirit—and that is exactly what the filters I set in my life help me do.

. . . A barbarous noise environs me
Of owls and cuckoos, asses, apes, and dogs.
— JOHN MILTON

A LIFE IN THE FILTERED SUN

Here are some of the specific filters I have set for what comes into my life. Again, they may be very different from the filters you choose, but perhaps they can be helpful examples.

First, I don't do "headline news" or subscribe to any form of "up-to-the-minute" cable coverage. I have decided that any information I receive about what is going on in the world around me will come to me only through low-tech means, especially through well-written, intelligent news journals and magazines. In addition, as a matter of policy, I try to avoid any form of sensationalized news. I avoid even newspapers and magazines that focus on scandals, and I steer clear of any form of reporting that focuses primarily on crimes and violence. Because the amount of time I have for gathering information is limited, I take special care to be sure that my news sources feature thoughtful analysis rather than gossip and sensationalism.

The deliberate refusal to be constantly up-to-the-minute on every detail of the latest mass murder or celebrity divorce seems somehow un-American to some people. But I believe this is because we as a culture have developed an unhealthy addiction to immediate information and sensationalistic accounts of disturbing events.

We have bought into two assumptions that I believe are inherently false. First, we assume that if we know what is going on as soon as possible (even as it is happening in some cases), we will somehow have more control of the situation. I don't believe this is true. As far as I can see, my knowing about an earthquake in a distant country just minutes or hours after it happens doesn't help me, nor does it help the people in that country. Out of human compassion we all feel the sting of such catastrophes, and many of us nurture a desire to be of some help. But there is usually plenty of time to do so in the ensuing weeks and months after a disaster. My desire to contribute to rescue relief does not depend on my knowing all the horrific details of that disaster within an hour of its occurrence.

A second faulty assumption many of us make is that we can somehow lead cleaner, more decent lives by staying abreast of the latest dirt that surrounds us. As far as I can see, knowing sordid details about the latest child abuse incident does little to help anyone be a better parent. In my view, it can only increase fear and anxiety, an obviously unhealthy atmosphere for the home.

Here's a question to ask yourself: Is there one sensational headline event of a year ago that is still front-page news? Usually the answer is no. The gruesome murder trial gets displaced by political scandals, which are then overshadowed by gang violence. And each sensational event is typically presented in a hyped-up manner designed to boost broadcast ratings and newsstand sales.

Does knowing about any of this as soon as it happens and having every violent, horrifying detail magnified and discussed time and time again throughout your day really improve your quality of life or help you fulfill your responsibilities as a citizen of the world? For me, the answer is again no. That is why I have set a filter to protect myself from constant, unnecessary, and sensationalist news input.

That doesn't mean I don't know what's happening in the world. In fact, I have found that focusing on low-tech, intelligently written forms of news gathering allows me to be better in tune with what is really happening than my friends who spend hours each day glued to a cable news service. This is because "up-to-the-minute" coverage tends to deliver information in scattered, fragmentary form, while the written coverage I prefer provides fuller, more complete analysis. I find that my way of "doing news," in fact, helps me interact more effectively with the issue at hand, develop a more informed opinion, and even find better ways to become involved on the occasions when I can be of some direct help.

The only real drawback I have discovered to establishing my news filter is that I occasionally feel momentary discomfort from feeling out of the loop. Perhaps I'll fail to recognize a name dropped in conversation. But all I have to do is ask for an explanation. And I have been amazed at just how rare an experience this is. The amount of news that bombards each of us every day is so vast that even a very strong filter will not keep it all out—any more than the thickest tree will keep all the sunshine away from the ground.

Another filter I set has more to do with the company I keep than with what I hear and see. Because my family is my priority, my social involvements tend to be relatively limited. As a result, I don't feel I have much extra time to spend with acquaintances whose outlook on life is chronically negative or cynical.

This is not because I don't *like* negative people. I, for one, find all kinds of people fascinating, even those whose basic take on life is that the glass is almost empty. I enjoy hearing their stories and wondering what makes them tick. And it goes without saying that I would not avoid a close friend or family member who is going through a down period and needs my encouragement and support.

When it comes to casual friends and social acquaintances, however, I do choose to limit my contact with negative people. It's too easy for me to slip into habits of thinking that pull me down—fear, distrust, suspicion. It's too

easy to fall into the habit of talking about people behind their back or thinking the worst of them. Within the bounds of basic civility and tact, therefore,
I avoid those who seem to choose these attitudes and behaviors on a regular
basis. When I do socialize, I intentionally seek out companions who enjoy
good conversation and positive activities; people who, like me, believe that
life still offers a lot to be hopeful about and that many of the problems in the
world are fixable.

SETTING YOUR FILTERS

Once again, the particular filters I have chosen for my life may not work
for you. Your filters will depend on your particular circumstance.

If you are an international relief worker, you really need to know about
the earthquake in that distant land. If your calling is to work with sick and/or
emotionally needy people, avoiding negative people will probably not be a
good decision for you.

Nevertheless, I suspect there are areas in your life where you could build
in more joy by filtering out certain kinds of input.

Even if you are not quite ready to turn off the twenty-four-hour news
channel, I do think you might profit from examining the sources that bring
you news and the ways in which they bring it. Instead of remaining
constantly "on call" to receive the latest-breaking information, you might
consider setting aside certain times when you will seek out the information
for yourself. By their very nature, written sources tend to be a little less
"noisy" and crisis-oriented than video or audio sources, so you might give
some thought to getting your news from a good daily newspaper or a weekly
news journal. Whatever medium you choose, though, I urge you to give some
thought to the sources that bring you information. Are they reliable? Is the
information they report balanced? Do they tell you what you need to know
about important issues or simply stir up your anxiety and stress and leave you
feeling helpless and confused?

If your mailbox is full of junk that wastes your time, you can set a filter
by taking steps to get yourself off mailing lists. Donna Otto, an organization-
al counselor, recommends writing and copying a simple form letter requesting
removal from a mailing list and sending it in response to every prepaid adver-

tisement envelope you receive. She did this for herself and recorded the results over a six-month period: more than 80 percent of the merchants she mailed the letter to took her off their lists. An even simpler form of filtering junk is to keep a recycling bin next to the mailbox. It doesn't take much experience to recognize those junk mail envelopes. Don't even open them—recycle them immediately. Once in a while you may make a mistake, but chances are you won't.

Once you begin the strategy of installing these simple filters, you'll begin to see many more opportunities. Perhaps you can install insulation in your home to filter out noise from the street. Perhaps you can make a simple decision not to answer the telephone or the doorbell during dinner or your personal quiet time.

Any of these strategies can serve the larger purpose of softening the impact of too much input in your life. It can quiet you, rest you, free your mind to make more decisions that bring you closer to joy.

And then, of course, when you go out in the harsh sun, be sure to wear a hat—to filter the real sunshine and keep your daylight soft and beautiful.

FILTERING WHAT GOES OUT

Up to now, though, we have been speaking primarily of filtering external stimuli—establishing protective barriers against the overwhelming information that comes to us from the outside. But I am increasingly coming to understand that, if I want to live a truly joyful, light-filled life, the filtering process must be internal as well.

It's not enough, for instance, to limit the amount and kinds of information I let myself read or listen to or observe. If I truly want to live peacefully and positively, I need to pay attention to what goes on in my head and heart and also to what proceeds from my mouth and shows in my actions. I am learning it is not only possible, but also enormously helpful, to discipline my thoughts, to focus the workings of my mind on what is uplifting. I am learning to mind my tongue as well, to limit my comments to what is truly helpful to myself and others.

This is certainly not a new notion. Centuries before Norman Vincent Peale started extolling the virtues of positive thinking, wise men and women observed that our intellects and our imaginations and our emotions have the power to shape the person we become—and that to a large degree we have control of these things. We may not be able to control what occurs to us, the passing thoughts and feelings that flicker like lightning through our brains. But we can control what we allow to remain. And we can certainly control what we allow ourselves to do or say as a result of these thoughts and feelings.

Here's a personal example. Say a person my company hired to do a job has simply not lived up to his or her end of the bargain and has not completed the job satisfactorily in a given period of time. This failure threatens to jeopardize a project that is very dear to my heart. Naturally, when I discover what is going on, I experience feelings of anger and frustration. My first thoughts run along the lines of blame—that person should never have promised what he could not deliver. I also find myself worrying about what this situation will do to a carefully planned upcoming vacation.

Now, all of these responses come to me immediately and involuntarily; they are a simple, natural reaction to the situation. From that point on, though, I have some choices about the thoughts and feelings I allow to shape my response. I have control as well over the things I say both to and about the person who failed in the job. I have control over what I will do next.

What determines these choices? First, they are shaped by prior decisions I have made about what is important. They are shaped by the central focus of my life and by the goals and priorities that spring from that central focus. After that, though, my choices will be shaped by the filters I have set up for my thought processes, my speech, and my actions.

For me, these inner filters are set to avoid stewing in anger, wallowing in frustration, or casting blame on others. I have found that doing any of these things robs me of my peace and adds to my stress just as surely as watching televised newscasts of the latest violence in our city. I have also set a filter against trying to even the score with those who have wronged me and against speaking ill of another person.

So what do I do once I've had a little time to respond to the situation?

First, I try to understand what is going on. What were the reasons for the failure? Were there ways in which I contributed to the problem?

Next, I try to avoid casting blame and to focus instead on how the situation can be remedied. I avoid sitting with my colleagues, complaining about this particular person, or immediately assuming the worst—that the person is unsuited to further tasks for the company in the future. To do so would be counterproductive as well as contradictory to my choice of filter. Instead, I try to focus my energy on what must be done to rescue the project that is in danger and on ways to affirm future success for the individual in question.

My aim is to walk forward, internal filters in place, and to have an influence that is beneficial to all concerned.

FILTER FALLACIES

It doesn't always work perfectly, of course.

No filters can protect an individual from ever thinking negative thoughts, speaking ill of others, or engaging in harmful actions. I am human, after all. I am acutely aware that I make mistakes; in fact, that is one reason I have established the internal filter against dwelling on blame and recrimination.

But I have found that the filters I have established in my life—both external and internal—have saved me enormous amounts of energy and freed me to fill my life with positive influences. These preselected judgments about general categories of influence I don't want in my life save me the ongoing stress of having to decide each one on an individual basis.

Thus, I say, "I don't do headline or sensational news." That doesn't mean I never encounter that kind of reporting. It does mean that I save myself hours each week by not sitting through repetitious reports on the current big story. I can relax in my knowledge that what is important will still be around in a day or two and that I'll hear about it.

Similarly, I try to avoid accusation and guilt and self-pity. That doesn't mean I never let an accusatory comment slip out or that I don't occasionally wallow in regrets or self-generated sob stories. It does mean I save myself hours of frustration trying to determine who did what to whom. I try not to focus on blame or justice or retribution, but on future life-affirming options.

Most important, when I say "I don't do negativity," I don't mean "I don't do reality."

How can anybody not do reality? That's like saying, "I don't do sunshine." Except, perhaps, for those white catfish that live in caves, all creatures live under the inescapable influence of the sun. And we all do reality.

If you are going to stare at truth,
if you don't want the birthing of agony to tear you apart,
give it a hard look only when you are in the middle of celebrating life. . . .
Cry in the night . . . but also rejoice.
— KAREN BURTON MAINS

I suppose that some people do use external and internal filters as a form of denial—hiding from reality by refusing to listen to the facts or think about them or talk about them. They filter out needs they truly should attend to, demands that truly apply to them.

A person who is out of shape, for instance, may consciously or unconsciously filter out input that reminds him of the reality that poor diet and lack of exercise is likely to shorten his life. A person whose finances have begun to spin out of control may avoid answering the phone or going to the mailbox and also, perversely, resist seeking any kind of financial help. A person whose marriage is in trouble may proceed as if nothing were wrong, refusing to talk about or even acknowledge the presence of a problem.

Even then, reality eventually gets through. Human filters were never meant to keep reality at bay, and sooner or later the truth about living in a body or handling financial responsibilities or managing a marriage will come crashing in.

And that, of course, is why filtering should never be confused with denial—although, being human, I've been guilty of denial from time to time, just like everybody else! Not long ago, in fact, Nanette and I had to take the painful step of facing up to a reality we had been trying to ignore, the fact that a housing situation we had arranged for a friend just wasn't working out. For several weeks we persisted in "thinking positive" when what we needed to do was take action and change the situation.

We eventually had to take action on the problem, wishing with all our hearts that we hadn't spent quite so much time denying that it was a problem.

But properly maintained filters will actually bring you closer in touch with the deepest form of reality—the truth that exists beneath the confused tangle of daily influences.

TRUE REALITY

In fact, one of my main purposes in relying on filters is to shut down the noise that prevents me from hearing the truth, the mental confusion that steers me away from the way things really are. I set filters to keep out the distractions that prevent me from focusing on the true reality behind the onslaught of facts and feelings and partial truths that fly at me constantly and flit through my brain. And the bedrock truth I usually return to when I manage to shut out all those other noises is the same truth that leads me to set those filters in the first place—the big-picture truth of what life in this world is really about.

One of the most common confusions, I believe, in this whole issue of what to let into our lives, is a confusion about what reality is. The common tendency is to equate reality with "cold, hard facts"—harsh truths like death and taxes that are supposed to bring us up short and nip our dreams in the bud. There really is a widespread assumption that "reality" is by definition negative and ugly.

I believe that is simply wrong, a tragic fallacy. Any truly objective observation of this world will reveal that reality is far bigger than any set of cold, hard facts and any rude awakening, no matter how painful.

Yes, suffering is part of reality. Yes, life includes disappointment and betrayal and fear and failure and tragedy. Yes, bad things happen to good people. The filters in my life should never be set to eliminate all the negative— nor could they do it.

But as I see it, pain and disappointment and betrayal and failure and tragedy are only part of the picture, and allowing myself to dwell on these things only sets a negative filter that can prevent me from seeing the bigger, brighter, more varied and beautiful whole.

For life—any life, even the saddest—holds elements of joy as well as

suffering. Life, if you have eyes to see the whole picture, brims with meaning, with purpose. It offers second chances. It offers courage and strength and humor to cope with the inevitable negatives. For every mean and hateful act we hear about on the news, there are a thousand kindnesses that went unreported. When we get things in perspective, the almost indescribable beauty of our world will overwhelm the occasional glimpses of the sordid and ugly.

Yes, tornadoes and violent thunderstorms are reality. But so are warm, breezy summer days.

Disappointment and disillusionment are realities, but so are joyful surprises.

Yes, death is an inescapable reality. But so is the miracle of birth.

When I make the choice to establish filters in my life, it's for the express purpose of softening the glare so I can see *more* than pain and suffering, turning down the noise so I can focus on the still, small voice that reminds me everything will be all right.

I desire to keep a clear view of reality in all its multifaceted glory, but especially its pulsing, brimming, life-giving vitality. Because I am what I eat and read and listen to and say and think, I want to take in whatever will make me most healthy in body, mind, and spirit.

When that happens, filter or not, I really will be living in the sunshine.

And the joy in my heart will make the world a brighter place.

When I filter the sunshine in my life,
I bask in the light of a transforming and inspiring reality.

LIGHTPOSTS
FOR LIVING

SIX

A NECESSARY BEAUTY

LIVING IN THE LIGHT OF THE LOVELY

Happily may I walk.
May it be beautiful before me.
May it be beautiful behind me.
May it be beautiful below me.
May it be beautiful above me.
May it be beautiful all around me.
In beauty it is finished.
— NAVAJO NIGHT CHANT

She walked up to me at the gallery opening with a painting under one arm and a twinkle in her eye.

"I want you to know," she said with a smile, holding up the painting, "that this is really a dishwasher."

I raised an eyebrow. The painting in question was one of mine. To me, it bore no resemblance to a kitchen appliance.

Then she explained.

"I really need a dishwasher," she said. "My old one broke months ago, and I've been saving up for a new one. I had just about saved enough. But then I came in here and saw this painting, and I just had to have it. Just looking at it makes me happy. So there goes my dishwasher money. But that's all right. I can wash my dishes by hand as long as I have something beautiful to look at."

By now I was smiling, too. I'm always glad when one of my paintings finds a loving home. But my happiness was mostly directed at what she was saying about the importance of beauty in her life.

She was demonstrating through her actions—through her *sacrifice*—something I believe with all my heart: Beauty is not a luxury.

The need for beauty may not be quite as basic as our need for food, water, and shelter, but it ranks not far below these basic needs. The human soul hungers for beauty—to experience beauty, and to create beauty—just as powerfully as our bodies hunger for food. Or souls wither when they are beauty-deprived. We need, in the words of a classic song, both bread *and* roses.

Why is beauty so important? Because we derive energy and motivation from beautiful sights, beautiful sounds, beautiful words and ideas, and beautiful environments. Beauty is food for the soul, balm to the spirit, inspiration for anything worthwhile we do with our lives.

And yes, it's true that joy is an inside job, that we can't depend on outside circumstances, even the presence of beauty, for our happiness. But just as the body grows and flourishes on a healthy diet, our joy can grow and flourish when fed a steady diet of beauty.

I am convinced that steeping ourselves in beauty is one of the most practical strategies we can adopt to build radiant joy into every minute of our day. In fact, I am so convinced of this that I have committed my life to sharing little glimpses of beauty with others in any and every way possible, with whatever talents I may possess. I believe this is a worthy goal, a high calling. It's a pursuit every bit as valuable as manufacturing even the most practical items—yes, even a dishwasher!

THE BEAUTIFUL OUTDOORS

So how do we do it? How do we build more beauty into our days?

The most important first step I can think of is a step outdoors. Gaze up into the skies. Smell the heady perfume of flowers and grasses. Feel the evening breeze or the warm midday sunshine on your face. Pick up a water-polished stone and relish the cool smoothness in your hand.

This is the place where the experience of beauty begins—the rich and

complex and abundant beauty of God's wondrous creation.

We are, after all, a part of nature. Our status as beings who breathe fresh air and live an organic existence predisposes us to respond to natural beauty. We need the air, the sunshine, the wind, and the trees in order to feel at peace. Returning to nature is a way of connecting ourselves with the natural us, of grounding ourselves in the rich soil of reality. Natural light and fresh air have the power to restore us to who we are, to a sense of completeness. I find it hard to contemplate a truly joyful life that is not connected intimately with the outdoors.

My artistic mentor, Glenn Wessels, discovered this fundamental, connective power of nature relatively late in his life. At the beginning of his career, like most young artists of the 1920s, Glenn expressed his artistic ideas largely through abstract forms. Although he was a supreme lover of nature, a good friend of the great landscape photographer Ansel Adams, his approach to art was essentially intellectual. His paintings consisted of explorations of color and shape that had much more to do with the world inside his head than with the world outside his window.

But then, when he was in his seventies, something happened to Glenn — first an accident, then a revelation. While on an outing in the mountains, Glenn suffered a fall that left him crippled. He could walk only very slowly, with a walker. Almost instantly his world became smaller. But as a direct result, he found himself more vividly attuned to the world around him. As he moved along at his snail's pace, he would find himself noticing the delicate structures of moss, the patterns of sunlight on a path.

Then one day Glenn accepted an invitation to go on a picnic with friends. Because of his injury, he elected to stay behind while they went on a hike. He lay on the ground under a tree, gazing up at the patterns of leaves and twigs against an achingly blue sky. Then Glenn Wessels experienced a revelation that changed his life and his painting and eventually, because he was my teacher, my painting as well.

It was a transcendent moment. Lying there under that tree, Glenn saw more clearly than ever before the fundamental, seminal, and almost heart-stopping beauty of the created world. And from that moment on, Glenn Wessels's work became a celebration of nature. He began with a painting of those leaves against that sky. From there he went on to paint intricate, intimate landscapes—studies of rocks and trees and moss and leaves. He observed intently, he drank in the beauty of the outdoors, and a new body of work began to flow from his renewed love for nature.

This was the man, the artist, who came to live practically next door to me when I was a teenager. He agreed to teach me in return for help around the studio. And during the next few years, as I cleaned brushes and stretched canvas, I also learned the lesson that Glenn himself had learned, that artists have discovered and rediscovered through the centuries.

The first beauty the world has to offer is in nature. The deepest beauty, the most inspiring beauty, the most elemental beauty, begins in the fields and forests and mountaintops. It is to be found in garden paths and desert look-outs and highland trails and wave-swept beaches. It lurks in tiny niches of rock and shouts in a sweep of sky.

If you want beauty in your life, in other words, you simply have to go out-doors from time to time. I try to make a point of spending at least an hour of every day outdoors—rain or shine.

You don't have to travel long distances to revel in natural beauty, although I love to visit spots where it assumes its most dramatic forms. It's not necessary to reside in a certain part of the country, although I find con-tinual inspiration and energy from the beautiful area where I live.

All you have to do, most of the time, is to go outside and look at the sky.

Take a walk in your neighborhood, or visit a nearby park. I am constantly amazed at how few people take advantage of public parks and gardens. If you have the time or the inclination, cultivate your own little private park—a lawn or garden or even a couple of big pots planted with flowers and herbs.

Ample and abundant beauty can probably be found in your own neighborhood, but expanding your horizons will help you become more acutely aware of the beauty nature has to offer. Visit a national park or wilderness area you've never been to. Seek out a Japanese garden or an arboretum. Dress appropriately and enjoy a walk in the rain or the snow. When you travel, make a point of experiencing and appreciating different kinds of landscapes—prairie, desert, mountains, even rain forest.

Sometimes you can heighten your experience and appreciation of natural beauty by participating in outdoor activities you may never have tried. Taking walks and riding bikes are wonderful ways to experience the beauty of the world around you. Even with simple equipment, an overnight campout can usually be managed with minimal problems and maximum enjoyment. Or try interacting in some way with what you're experiencing—write down your thoughts in a journal, take along a camera, or (my favorite) bring along a sketchpad or some paints.

Any of these activities can be wonderful ways to heighten your experience of natural beauty. But they shouldn't be your only excuses to go outside. You don't need an excuse! The beauty of nature is its own reward. Just being there is enough to transform you and fill your life with hope, serenity, and joy.

This is exactly the lesson I have learned from my practice of plein air painting. *Plein air* essentially means "fresh air" or "al fresco"—this is the kind of painting that is done outdoors, directly from nature. Although I had always enjoyed working outdoors, I took up this practice seriously a number of years ago. I meant it as a kind of discipline, a way of studying nature that I thought would be beneficial in the creation of my studio paintings. I took some pains to design the perfect portable easel, and then I renewed my experience in mobile painting.

Since then, I have learned a lot that has helped my studio work. I have learned about the fluctuations of natural light, about the forms and composition of rocks and trees and water. But what I have learned best in this process is simply to savor the breathtaking beauty of the natural world.

I discovered that while in the past I had often traveled through nature, hiking or running or flying a kite, I had rarely taken the time patiently to learn its lessons. Plein air painting gave me the excuse to sit, often for hours at a time, and observe the beauty of creation. Now, even when I'm not painting, I have formed the habit of quietly absorbing the natural world, gazing in awestruck wonder at the beauty that surrounds me. Learning this habit has been one of the keys to a joy that, like nature, renews itself season by season.

FURNISH YOUR LIFE WITH BEAUTY

The world of sun and sky and ocean and trees is a dependable, almost inexhaustible source of beauty in any life. But I don't live outdoors. Neither do you, most likely. Aside from occasional camping trips, most of us spend the bulk of our time indoors, at home or at school or at work.

We need beauty in those places, too, if we want to lead joy-filled lives. We need to surround ourselves and our families with objects and ideas and activ-

ities that please and excite our senses, that make us smile, that provide a soothing balm of comfort for our days.

I believe, in fact, that the more we do to furnish our daily lives with beauty—hanging it on our walls, spreading it on our floors, stocking our shelves and setting our tables with it—the closer to joy we'll find ourselves living.

I am not just talking about choosing paint and hanging wallpaper, but about shaping the total atmosphere of your home and your workspace, wrapping beauty around yourself through the colors and textures you choose, the objects you place on walls and floor, the music you play, the bedding you sleep in nightly, even the dishes that frame the meals you eat.

You don't need to be a professional decorator to wrap your home in this kind of beauty. You don't need to hire a professional, either, or to follow a set of rules. You certainly don't need expensive fabrics or furniture or decorative items—and not everything has to match. All you have to do is be conscious of the spaces around you and begin shaping them into environments that to your own eye are lovely and inviting.

Although this challenge of filling a space with beauty is one that men sometimes show little interest in, I have found that creatively shaping my home and work environment can be as fulfilling as any typically "male" activity I'm involved in. Whenever my wife and I travel, we keep our eyes open for that ideal accent piece to go over the mantel, that little painting or print to fill the blank wall above the light switch. And, though the objects that fill our home are eclectic and often unrelated, a theme of warmth and comfortable family living has emerged over the years as we have put together each room.

Designer William Morris, whose ideas of beauty and simplicity revolutionized home design around the turn of the century, once said, "If you want a golden rule that will fit everybody, this is it: Have nothing in your houses that you do not know to be useful, or believe to be beautiful." That is precisely what we try to do in our home. In most cases, in fact, we try to fill our living and working spaces with objects that are both beautiful *and* useful.

A thing of beauty is a joy for ever:
Its loveliness increases; it will never
Pass into nothingness.
—JOHN KEATS

༈

WINDOWS TO BEAUTY

What specifically do we do to bring beauty into our rooms?

First, because we share a deep love of art (and also, obviously, because I happen to be a painter) our walls are covered with pictures. I hang my own paintings in our home because, as immodest as this may sound, I really enjoy my own work! I guess that's one of my primary reasons for painting—to capture on canvas the beauty that inspires me, the kinds of worlds I am drawn to. But we also have paintings and prints by artists whose work we have enjoyed, sometimes since childhood.

We don't make any attempt to make sure that the colors or the subjects match. We don't say to ourselves, "We need a painting with blue in it to match the color of this couch." We simply surround ourselves with paintings we love. To me paintings are more than mere decorations; they are windows of beauty that allow our hearts to soar.

Whatever objects create that effect in your heart will serve the purpose of furnishing your home with beauty. However, on behalf of my colleagues, the artists of this world (and at the risk of sounding self-serving), I would like to make a case for including pictures in your decor—as opposed to decorating only with dried flowers, antique kitchen implements, textile wall hangings, and the like.

There's certainly nothing wrong with any form of decorative touch. And hanging interesting objects can be a creative godsend, especially when budgets are tight. But there is something about a well-crafted picture, whether a painting, a numbered print, or just an inexpensive reproduction, that provides something extra, a sort of escape hatch into a world of the imagination. I would encourage you to look for art that reminds you of places you want to be, things you want to do, or times you have been happy. Look for pictures that call forth the best in you, that make you want to live a happier, simpler, more meaningful life. You won't regret buying such a piece, even if you have to stretch to afford it.

My wife and I did exactly that many times in our leaner years. We made the difficult decision to purchase a one-of-a-kind work of art instead of some other much-needed item. And we have never regretted doing without a newer car or fancier clothing in order to surround ourselves with an ever-growing collection of beautifully done paintings. Each piece in our collection is in our minds an heirloom.

Can you remember the pictures that hung on the walls of the home where you grew up—that print above the fireplace, that painting that always greeted you as you sat down to dinner? Art has a way of imprinting itself on you, of providing imagery that helps shape your outlook on the world. My children are growing up surrounded by the paintings in our home. They are comfortable with each work. Someday, we hope, our paintings will hang on their walls—and their children's walls—a priceless heritage of beauty and joy. I am often told by collectors that my paintings and prints provide the same kind of heritage for their families. How marvelous to think that, in some small way, my work as an artist will enrich the lives of future generations!

Beauty from Life

But paintings are not the only objects that help me furnish our home and studio and offices with beauty. I find great joy in beautifying our environment with objects that are not only lovely in themselves but that have personal meaning to us as well.

Our appreciation for the beauty of timeless, well-worn objects has inspired us to fill our home with old items—even inexpensive ones garnered from garage sales and junk shops. Over the years we have accumulated some lovely old furniture, some wonderful pieces of glass or bronze, plus a few objects that are beautiful because they are historic oddities. For example, a handmade wicker and iron miniature sleigh accents the area where we read to our children at night—a perfect caddy for the hundreds of tattered children's books we've accumulated since our first child was born.

To nurture our love for the outdoors, we open our windows wide for a full view of trees and grass and flowers. In fact, with rare exceptions, we don't even have drapes or blinds. We also bring the outdoors in by raising houseplants and proudly displaying the treasures we have discovered on our walks together—leaves, wildflowers, interesting rocks and shells from the beach. In addition, we extend our home life into the open air by decorating and furnishing our patio and yard with benches, tables, even little sculptures.

We love to take our morning tea outdoors, where its fragrant warmth tastes even better. When possible, we also eat in the open air. For us, the indoor-outdoor lifestyle heightens our perception of the beauty all around us.

Travel is important to us as well, so we love to adorn our home with mementos from places we've enjoyed. The porcelain plates we collected in various countries of Europe, the odd little stool we dis-covered in an Irish antique shop, the vintage books we hunted up in tiny London bookshops—all these things are full of beautiful memories to us, and we love to display them in our home.

Books, in fact, are an important presence in our home and in my studio as well. They line the shelves, and they collect in piles around my comfortable chair (a distinct compromise for Nanette, who is more inclined to find beau-ty in order). And although many of the volumes are inherently beautiful—I love the way they combine beautiful thoughts and ideas with the visual beauty of design—they are by no means just for show. We read to each other regularly from volumes of prose and poetry. We pore over the pictures. We handle the books and enjoy the feel of rich paper and well-worn bindings. In our home, we like to be surrounded by beautiful words.

A TREAT FOR THE SENSES

Furnishing a home in beauty, you see, is not just a matter of surrounding yourself with visual beauty. Beauty enters your heart through all the senses, and I believe the beauty grows stronger when more than one of the senses is involved.

Beautiful sound, for instance, adds a wonderful layer of tranquillity to a joyful ambience. In other words, a beautiful home *sounds* good. A Mozart sonata or a flowing fountain or a tinkling wind chime—any sound that is beautiful to *you* — can provide the kind of joyful ambience you prefer, whether it is a soothing atmosphere for rest and quiet talk or something lively for exercise or chores.

Conversation can be music to the ears as well. The laughter of my children is one of my favorite sounds, as comforting as a warm mug of cocoa. Even in quiet times, my soul is inspired by the gentle music of living. My wife turning the page of a magazine, my daughter scribbling in a coloring book, even the hollow ticking of our family grandfather clock — all these sounds of a peaceful home at rest are beautiful to my ears.

Even more elemental to furnishing a home with beauty, I believe, is filling it with beautiful aromas. Have you ever noticed how a single whiff of a familiar fragrance has the power to carry you instantly back to your childhood? The sense of smell seems to be powerfully connected to emotion and to memory. That is why beautiful smells contribute so strongly to an experience of beauty.

In our family, my wife is the expert at filling our home with beautiful aromas — a wonderful stew simmering in a crockery pot or a banana bread baking in the oven. She has taught me to appreciate more deeply the rich fragrance of a rose, the homey smell of vanilla, the fresh scent of rain through an open window.

Because she loves to cook, Nanette also fills our home with wonderful tastes. Dinner at our home, whether simple and homespun or elaborate and elegant, is always a memorable experience. I have learned from my wife to appreciate the old-fashioned art of setting a beautiful table to present the meals she lovingly creates.

I am the one in the family, on the other hand, who seems to appreciate most deeply the wonder of touch — the experience of beautiful textures and tactile forms. I am a hands-on person when it comes to experiencing the world. I like to pick things up, run my fingers over them, experience the way they feel. So I fill my home and my studio with objects that are nice to touch — a granite stone fireplace, small bronze sculptures, worn wooden antiques, textured fabrics.

To me, there's something about the sense of touch that is directly connected to creativity. I remember an old Sherlock Holmes movie in which the detective was wandering about his study, pondering a particularly complex problem. He would walk over to the desk, pick up an inkwell, hold it, study it, put it down. Then he would pick up a violin bow, run his fingers down the long shaft, caress the horsehair, put it down. All the time you could practically see the wheels in his mind turning, the ideas being processed. The very act of handling objects seemed to awaken his creative abilities.

I believe this is true of most people, especially children. And that is one reason we have deliberately planned our house to be a hands-on experience. Very little is off limits to our children, although we set aside certain areas for enthusiastic play and other areas for quieter enjoyment. We encourage our little ones to touch, to feel, to enjoy the world they live in.

We find that living with beauty in this hands-on way somehow makes it more personal. We're not just looking at beauty or appreciating it from a distance; we are making it ours. We are letting beauty touch us, change us, inspire us, fill us with joy.

And that, after all, is the fundamental purpose of beauty.

THE EYE OF THE BEHOLDER

Simply put, beauty is found in anything that delights the senses, nourishes the soul, fires the imagination. Beautiful objects, ideas, even beautiful people all share the power to lift the spirits and motivate creativity while at the same time soothing the soul. Beauty has "presence" to it, an ability to command notice either subtly or quietly.

These qualities, of course, are highly subjective. Beauty truly is, as the old adage has it, in the eye (and mind) of the beholder. For reasons as diverse as the human psyche, what one person finds supremely beautiful may fail to elicit a second look from another. One person in a museum will be drawn to a room of Russian icons while another heads straight for the Impressionists. One will stand rapt before a seventeenth-century Flemish interior while another gazes upward in delight at a twentieth-century mobile . . . and yet another strolls outside to walk among the flowers in the museum garden.

When I enter a gallery that carries my paintings, I am often intrigued by the way the pieces affect different types of people. A well-dressed socialite may gravitate to a rustic mountain cabin scene. A laborer from a local assembly plant (still wearing his work uniform) may stand, utterly entranced, before a painting of a lush garden scene. Some collectors tell me, "I love your seascape paintings best," while others purchase only cityscapes. People who've never been near England will tell me they particularly enjoy my re-creations of distinctly British thatched-roofed cottages. And inevitably I receive dozen of requests every year for subjects I rarely or never paint: "When are you going to paint a desert scene?" "How about an African subject?" "Have you ever been to the fjords of Norway to paint?"

Tastes vary, in other words. Perceptions of beauty vary. And I believe we should delight in this diversity of taste, just as we rejoice in the abundance of experiences that life has to offer. There is inherent beauty in the very breadth of human experience—and that, I believe, is cause for rejoicing. There is absolutely nothing wrong with saying "I like it because it's beautiful to me" or "It's beautiful to me because I like it." I have often heard the phrase "I don't know anything about art, but I know what I like," as though people feel a need to apologize for their personal tastes in artwork. There is no need to apologize. If you enjoy something and find it beautiful, that is reason enough to like it.

At the same time, I believe we grow toward joy as we learn to stretch our beauty muscles—to expand our understanding of what is beautiful. For some of us, this may mean learning to open our eyes to the beauty around us— beauty we might not recognize because we expect it in a different form.

Though we travel the world over to find the beautiful,
we must carry it with us, or we find it not.
— RALPH WALDO EMERSON

OPENING YOUR EYES TO BEAUTY

I have a friend who recently moved from East Tennessee to West Texas. For months now, she has struggled with acute homesickness for a landscape she considered beautiful, a place of lush vegetation and fold after fold of misty hills. When she first moved, she felt nothing but discouragement as she gazed over the flat, pale landscape of her new home. Even in the city, where trees are tenderly nurtured and lawns are coaxed carefully into greenness, she felt nothing but sadness that "everyone had to work so hard" for beauty.

But my friend is a person who believes that everything happens for a purpose, and she has been determined to find the purpose in her new situation. Part of this quest has involved looking for beauty even in a landscape that seemed ugly to her. And gradually, she says, she is learning to appreciate the unique beauties the prairie has to offer.

Mesquite trees, for instance, are gnarled and thorny and small, but they do display a lovely fringe of pale-green foliage. In late summer, the contrast between red soil, light-green mesquite, and bright-yellow sunflowers can be striking. Prairie skies provide a sweeping blue backdrop for the drama of passing thunderheads and the swoop of graceful, coral-breasted birds. And the carefully tended city trees, in contrast to the rugged country around, provide a welcome oasis.

"When I drive into my tree-shaded driveway," my friend tells me, "I find that I regard those trees with an intense appreciation I never felt for the trees back home. They seem like true treasures, worth every penny and every hour we spend to keep them healthy."

My friend still feels homesick for East Tennessee. She would move back if she could. In the meantime, though, she is finally beginning to see the beauty that surrounds her in a place she didn't think was beautiful at all. She is stretching her appreciation muscles, learning to look for beauty even in unlikely places. In the process, she is increasing her overall enjoyment for beauty.

The habit of looking for beauty wherever we are pays enormous dividends when it comes to the amount of energy and motivation beauty brings to our lives. It makes sense, doesn't it? The more beauty we are able to see, the more beauty will seem to surround us.

Sometimes this means learning to pay attention to details, letting our eyes focus on the wildflower in the junkyard. We can enjoy the beautiful shapes of vintage houses in a decaying neighborhood, the lovely lines of character on the face of an elderly friend, the snippet of parkland that refreshes a concrete cityscape.

At other times, opening our eyes to beauty really means opening our hearts and our imaginations, developing a vision for potential beauty. Sometimes we must learn to see not only the beauty that is present in a given situation, but also the beautiful possibilities that might be inherent but hidden.

A VISION FOR BEAUTY

When I face a blank canvas at the beginning of the painting process, I am already reveling in a glimpse of beauty I see in my mind. That vision is enough to carry me through the often-tedious processes of blocking out the picture, establishing the basic composition, and applying layer after painstaking layer of paint to prepare for the final touches that actually turn on the beautiful lights in the canvas.

Developing your ability to see such potential beauty is another way to build more beauty and joy into your life.

If you can look at a tumbledown ruin and envision a restored Victorian homestead, the house's potential beauty will enrich your life even as you gradually transform the rotten floorboards and peeling paint.

If you can picture yourself playing entrancing music on the violin, you can endure with good cheer the discord of your early lessons.

Whatever beautiful possibilities you can envision for yourself can sustain you when the beauty in your life seems in short supply or enrich the joy and beauty you are already experiencing.

It's a lovely, life-giving cycle. For what better way is there to nourish a vision for beauty than to expose yourself to beauty wherever you can find it? Feed your heart with beauty—outdoors, indoors, in your present life, in your memory—and you'll build a deeper, clearer vision for the beauty that can continue to fill your world, nourishing and enriching and coloring your life with joy.

I love old movies, including the musical classic *The Wizard of Oz*. This film

contains what must surely be one of the most transcendentally wonderful moments in all cinema—the moment when Dorothy's house, carried away from Kansas by a tornado, is deposited in the land of Oz. Up to this moment, the movie has been black and white. But when she steps out of her Kansas house into Oz, she also steps out from her black-and-white existence into a breathtaking Technicolor world.

Imagine the effect this moment must have had on movie audiences who were accustomed primarily to black-and-white films. This cinematic moment is a beautiful picture of the mental, emotional, and spiritual benefit that comes from opening your eyes to beauty in all its forms. For beauty is the quality that can transform the dull, black-and-white quality of our days into brilliant, rich, life-giving color.

After all, the world around us is a wondrous kingdom of delights, a far richer treat for the senses that any celluloid fantasy. We only need to open our eyes and ears, our hearts and souls to the beauty that surrounds us, the beauty inside us and the beauty that is yet to emerge. When we keep ourselves tuned to the beauty of our world, life itself becomes a joyous celebration of the senses, a song of praise to the wonder of all creation.

Steeping my life in beauty
brings color to my days and a song to my heart.

LIGHTPOSTS
FOR LIVING

SEVEN

A GLOWING HEARTH

LIVING CLOSE TO THE WARM LIGHT OF HOME

But every house where Love abides
And Friendship is a guest,
Is surely home, and home-sweet-home;
For there the heart can rest.
— HENRY VAN DYKE

Home. Is there is a more evocative word in all the English language?

Surely no other word (with the possible exception of *love*) has inspired more poetry or evoked more controversy over what it is and what it should be. Something about that simple little cluster of letters has the power to tug at our heartstrings, evoke vivid memories and strong emotions, stoke our imaginations, and stir our dreams.

Although I paint many subjects, from historical scenes to bustling cityscapes to sweeping mountain vistas, it is the paintings of homes—the little thatched-roof cottages or mountain cabins or rambling homesteads with their glowing windows—that seem to draw people like magnets. And I suppose it's no accident that these "home" pictures are popular, for they come from a place that is deep within my own heart. Ever since I was a boy, my dreams of travel and adventure have been balanced with a powerful sense of home, the vision of a warm center for all my roamings, the notion of a glowing hearth where I could retire after a hard day's work or a long day's journey to rest, to be renewed, to remind myself of who I am and what I love.

It is that hearth fire vision, I believe, that sparks my paintings of home and lends them their special appeal. And it is the same vision that leads me to make home a priority in my life, to invest my time and my energies to create a warm refuge for myself and my family, a place where we can all feel nurtured and cared for, safe and protected, free to be exactly who we are.

I call it making myself at home—and to me, it's a vital key to enduring joy.

Whether you're the type who spends your days puttering around the house, or whether your idea of happiness is a suitcase and the open road (I'm a little of both), you can still keep yourself grounded and rooted in joy by cultivating and nurturing a sense of home.

Making yourself at home is not so much a matter of financing a mortgage or putting up storm windows. It's not so much a matter of upholstering the sofa and setting out knickknacks and lighting a fire in the fireplace—though all these can be part of your experience of home.

Making yourself at home, as I see it, is first of all a matter of creating a resting place for your heart, a comfortable refuge, a place where your soul can take off its shoes, so to speak, and put up its feet.

It's a matter of understanding what home is, and what home can be—then throwing your heart into stoking the hearth fires into a golden glow that can truly warm your life.

Home is heaven for beginners.
— CHARLES PARKHURST

WHERE THE HEARTH IS

Today, I am blessed to live in a place that embodies my dreams of home— a comfortable, light-filled dwelling that rings with the laughter of children and shines with the warmth of its fireplace. Here, among a lived-in clutter of books and toys, our family sleeps and eats and plays and lives our life together. Here is the corner where Nanette curls up in her chair with a cup of tea and the opposite corner where I love to relax with a wonderful old book. Here is the hallway where the children practice their amazing feats of tumbling and the kitchen table that becomes the center for nightly homework. Here is the soft carpeting in the family room, just right for roughhousing or lounging around a game board.

Right next door is a smaller structure that also is dear to my heart, the remodeled cottage that houses my studio. This is my work home, as carefully planned and privately sacred as the family house. Here I am greeted daily by the comforting smell of the studio—a combination of turpentine and the worn leather of books and hunting-lodge furniture. Surrounding both home and studio is the green balm of lawn, warmed by the sun and shaded by an occasional oak or sycamore tree.

This place—the house and small studio beside it—is home for my heart. Though not overly fancy or formal, it is the culmination of years spent dreaming of a place to call our own. Nanette and I often declare, as we snuggle together on the family room sofa, that we never want to leave here. But even as we make that declaration, we have to remind ourselves that we also said that about the little house in the country where we lived many years ago, the first home we ever owned. Every one of the places where we've lived together, in fact, has taught us something new about the fine art of making ourselves at home.

Back in the early 1980s, for instance, home for Nanette and me was a very different kind of place—a tiny apartment in a low-income section of Pasadena, California. Our domain in those days consisted of two minuscule bedrooms—one for sleeping, one for painting—a run-down bathroom and cramped kitchen, and a living room barely big enough for secondhand easy chairs and the garage-sale stereo that provided music for our dwelling.

As I think back on that apartment, I can see it for the shabby little place it was. And yet we worked hard to transform it into a welcoming refuge. A small collection of my art school studies hung in one corner. Framed photos reminded us of our honeymoon and other travels we'd shared. The kitchen was both decorated and supplied with Nanette's assortment of old spice jars that held everything from colorful noodles to dried beans, all ready to be cooked up in her famous pots of goulash. And of course there was Nanette herself, my new bride, the love of my life. To me, her presence alone was enough to make that tiny rented space glow with beauty.

We had not been living in that apartment more than a few months when I was given the opportunity to travel to Alaska with a bush pilot who happened to be an art collector. This was a wonderful break for me, a chance to research a painting series I wanted to do on the grand landscapes of the north. It was also an invitation to indulge the wanderlust, the craving for adventure that has always been part of my personality. Alaska! I had always wanted to explore its untamed regions.

As the date approached, however, I found myself dreading the trip. It would be my first extended trip away from Nanette since we were married, and I had a hard time tearing myself away. Finally, with a good bit of hesitation, I boarded the plane.

Before I knew it, I was gazing out over the grandest, most awesome landscape I had ever seen. Yet as I soared above the treetops in the bush plane, as I set up my easel beside frozen lakes and marveled at the abundant wildlife, I felt my mind drifting back to our shabby little Pasadena apartment, drifting back toward home. Even amid the natural splendor of the Alaskan wilderness, I found myself hungry to return to four dingy rooms in Southern California.

I returned from my two weeks in the bush country a little worse for wear. My hands were covered with calluses from chopping wood for campfires. I was scratched and sunbaked and bug-bitten and worn, though also full of stories to tell and bubbling over with images waiting to be captured on canvas. But most of all I was ecstatically happy to be home, to return to my comfortable refuge where I could relax, regroup, heal, and get on with my day-to-day life.

It was then I realized something about home that I hadn't understood before. All my life, I had felt a tug between my dreams of home and my urge to roam, my drive to build a nest and my hunger to fly far from it. Now, as I curled up in my carefully crafted nest, I began to see that the two might not work against each other after all.

For it is the security that comes from truly being at home that gives one the courage and freedom to travel, to seek adventure. And it is the warmth and connection of home that gives meaning to the time I spend away, refining all my experience into the golden glow of memory to be treasured like a framed photograph on the wall.

Ever since that trip to Alaska, I have begun to think of my home as my anchor on earth, the place where my hearth fire keeps burning no matter where I go. It is the underlying stability that allows me to roam far, to take risks, to try new things, always knowing that the warm center of my life will hold me steady.

A PLACE TO CALL HOME

What do *you* think of when you hear the word *home*? What images and emotions come to mind? This is something to ponder, for these images and emotions have the power to shape your life, to give it meaning, to tell you who you are.

Chances are, the first thing that comes to mind when you think of home is a place. Your home is your house, your apartment, your condominium or mobile home. It is a physical collection of space and furnishings—perhaps the sunlit dining room you love, the cramped, gloomy bathroom you hate, the kitchen that isn't quite big enough, the front bedroom that is a perfect fit for your grandmother's antique sleigh bed.

Home for you is also, probably, a landscape, a setting as familiar to you as your own hands. Home is your front yard, with its clusters of zinnias and its ornamental mimosa tree and the patch of dead grass near the sidewalk. Home is your neighborhood, with its bumpy streets and clusters of children playing. It is also your part of the city, with its quaint little shops and the unattractive but useful shopping center. Home is your city or town, where you don't need a map to traverse the streets, and also the countryside that surrounds it, the memorized terrain of trees and hills—all the familiar images that define your territory on the earth.

Even if the images I suggest *aren't* familiar—if, for example, you live in an adobe hut beside a two-lane highway that slices across the heart of a desert—that merely underscores my point. To a larger degree than some of us like to think, we are shaped by the physical places where we live, by the concentric circles of structures and landscape that define our mortal home.

> *On the envelope the address was like this: It said: Jane Crofut; The Crofut Farm; Grover's Corners; Sutton County; New Hampshire; United States of America. . . . But listen, it's not finished: the United States of America; Continent of North America; Western Hemisphere; the Earth, the Solar System; the Universe; the Mind of God— that's what it said on the envelope. . . . And the postman brought it just the same.*
> —THORNTON WILDER

I believe the physical reality of home is a wonderful gift. Even our spiritual selves, after all, are housed in physical bodies. We all need a specific spot on this earth to call home, and we are created to respond to our physical environment. We can't help it. Certain locations speak to us, certain landscapes feel comfortable and familiar, certain places just feel like home.

Think about it. How many of your memories, happy or sad, are inextricably linked to physical places? How many memories of places you've lived vie for attention with memories of people you loved?

My mind and heart are full of these fragmented but vivid memories of places I lived even as a very small child—the cool damp earth under the hydrangea bushes in the backyard where I played, the pictures on the walls of our living room, even the bedroom, shared with my brother, with its odd hole in the wall. The hole had been punched by the knob of a door flung too energetically open. And for some reason this small cavity fascinated my brother and me; as little boys, we imagined a whole world, which we referred to as "germ city," living in the thin space behind the drywall.

I can still picture the floor plan of the house where I lived as an older child; even today, I could find my way around it in the dark. (Couldn't you do the same?) And the tiny mobile home where we used to visit my paternal grandmother is permanently etched in my memory. I could draw you a detailed portrait of that musty, cramped, but somehow comfortable and welcoming space. I could do the same for the hills around Placerville, my hometown, or for the roads we cruised on our bicycles.

Whatever else it might be, a home is unmistakably a place. It is the spot where our feet touch ground, the landscape that tells us where we belong. This gift of a physical setting for our lives is, I believe, something to rejoice in, to celebrate, to care for.

A PEOPLE'S HISTORY

And yet as anyone who has ever moved can testify, home is so much *more* than just a physical place. Almost any physical setting, in time, can come to feel like home, because your home is also your history.

It is the personal history, in fact, that actually transforms a physical setting into a home. A house is just a collection of bricks or boards until you have dinner there, then another dinner; until you sleep there and play there and laugh and cry there. The homeyness of that breakfast nook has more to do with your memories of morning coffee and late-night conversation than it

has to do with the distressed wooden tabletop and the comfortable padded seats. The restfulness of your bedroom has as much to do with memories of repainting the walls—and spilling the paint twice—as it does with the soothing color it is now.

The very acts of living, in other words, are the things that transform a house into a true home. As we go through the course of our days, waking, working, eating, doing homework, we are decorating our surroundings with memories—gradually, inescapably, creating our home.

Home is the place that'll catch you when you fall. And we all fall.
— BILLIE LETTS

Chances are, also, that we are doing these things with other people, for home and relationships are inextricably intertwined. Unless you're a hermit, your history will be built through interaction and connection with other people. In a sense, then, your relationships will be your home, and the process of making yourself at home also means nurturing those relationships. Every conversation, every cuddle, every kiss and caress, even every disagreement, adds another brushstroke to the picture of home you paint with the days and hours of your life.

Here, too, I believe your home will consist of ever-widening circles.

On the inside there is your family or your closest friendships, the people you relate to intimately on a daily basis. Usually these will be the people who live with you or who live very near. For me, this inner circle includes my wife and my children. It also encompasses my relationship with the person I know most intimately of all: myself.

Outside this intimate inner circle, the relationships that make up your home expand into a wider network. Your home, in a sense, is also the grocery clerk who always recognizes you, the friend who sits beside you at chapel or synagogue, the colleague whose office is next to yours. It is certainly your extended family, to the extent that you actually know each other and interact. Your mother who lives across town, your sister whom you e-mail regularly and visit when you can, your cousin whom you only recently met at a family reunion—all these are a part of who you are, and thus, in a sense, a part of your wider home.

A HOME TO CHERISH

Home, as I have described it thus far, is so much more than a place to hang your hat. It is a physical location, a personal history, and a set of relationships—all spreading out from the center of your life in ever widening circles of familiarity like warmth spreading out around a campfire.

But just as the way to warm up an entire circle of campers is to stir the fire they've gathered around, the most effective way to make yourself truly at home is to start at the center.

You begin with your three-bedroom brick house in the suburbs or your apartment atop an office building downtown. You begin with your habit of eating breakfast on the patio or your memories of a trip to the beach. You begin with your closest relationships—your friends, your spouse and children, even yourself.

And the first, most important thing you can do with any of these aspects of home is to cherish it.

Love your home—its physical space, its personal history, the relationships that define it. Celebrate home. Take care of its needs and pay some careful attention to its desires.

In practical terms, cherishing a home means first of all that you speak well of it. You look for its good points and share those with outsiders; you avoid holding up its faults to the glare of outside opinion.

I have long believed in this principle when it comes to people. (Airing out another person's dirty laundry in public is a surefire relationship killer.) But I have only recently begun to be aware of ways that speaking well of what you love can apply to a physical home as well. As Victoria Moran points out in her insightful book, *Shelter for the Spirit*, the way you speak of your home will actually affect the way that you and others see it:

> When people used to ask me how I liked my house, I'd say, "Well, it really doesn't get enough light and the buildings are too close on either side and there's this dark paneling. . . . " With that funereal recitation, I gave anyone who would listen instructions on precisely how to think poorly of my home. . . . So I quit. I started to talk instead about the shiny floors and the easy way the rooms connect with each

other. I talk about having breakfast on the front porch, and about the finished attic. . . . All these things that make me happy have been part of the house since the day we moved in. But only after seeing them from a new perspective did I begin to realize how much they add to my life.

Cherishing your home also means taking care of it. Anything worth loving is worth your time and attention, and that's true of your physical home, your memories, and your relationships. This may seem obvious, but I've observed that the people and places that are closest to us are often the first to be neglected during times of stress.

During a busy time at work, for instance, it would be easy to let the dishes pile up in the sink and to fall back on fast food in place of cooking dinner. Or we may let the lawn go or allow the children to watch more TV than is good for them or begin to skip our regular bedtime reading session. We may find ourselves cleaning only the rooms that "show," letting our private bedroom or bath become holding places for unfolded laundry and piles of magazines.

I'm not saying you should never let anything slide. Sometimes you can't avoid it. Sometimes you simply have to choose one priority over another.

Sometimes you even have to choose one element of home over another—neglecting the house, for instance, in favor of making a memory with the children. However, if you find yourself consistently putting your home life on hold while you tend to other "urgent" matters, it may be time to shift your priorities. You may need to simplify your life and make more time to cherish your home.

Yet another important way to cherish your home—perhaps the most important of all—is to cultivate an awareness of it. Anything familiar, even if it is precious, is easy to take for granted. You can cherish your house, your history, and relationships by doing everything you can to avoid that tendency. Practice looking at the rooms around you with joy and thankfulness, recognizing how blessed you are to have a place to live. Handle the mementos on the shelves. Gaze at the photographs. Be grateful. Appreciate.

Most of all, practice paying attention, really paying attention, to the people you love most dearly. Force yourself to listen even when you think you've heard the story before. Pay attention to ways your family may be changing, to new needs your loved ones may not yet be able to express. Notice the good they do and compliment them. Try to understand the negative acts. Cherish the people who make up your home, and you'll notice the hearth fires burn brighter than ever before.

One good way to foster the awareness of all the good in your home is actually to plan a house blessing—a time when you and your family and friends walk through the rooms of the home and offer specific prayers of thanksgiving and benediction. Your pastor or priest or rabbi may be happy to lead a time of blessing in your home. Or you may prefer to organize such a service as a simple gathering of those you love.

At the very least, pick a time when no one else is home and walk quietly through the rooms of your house or apartment. Focus on each one in turn, thinking of the ways it adds to your life. Your bathtub, for instance, offers you running water and cleanliness. A kitchen offers nourishment for both soul and body. A storage room gives the gift of order, a bedroom gives the gift of rest . . . and so on. Think also of the people who inhabit the rooms, of what they mean in your life and the memories you have made together. Take the time to be grateful. Then, if you wish, offer it all, even the walls and floors and the ceiling, to God's care. I believe you'll find that this time of blessing provides you with a heightened awareness and a deeper love of the gift that is your home.

MAKE IT YOURS

No house, however cherished, is perfect. No personal history is devoid of mistakes. No one in your family is without flaws—including you. That means that in every home there is room for improvement. More accurately, in every home there is room for *personalization*. The setting that shapes you can also be shaped by you. A vital part of making yourself at home is altering both the physical space and the emotional atmosphere to suit the personalities and needs of the people who inhabit it.

To me, this process of shaping is part of the joy of having a home base. I love to be involved in the ongoing process of customizing my physical space to build in an ever-deepening sense of comfort and joy. For example, when one of the children develops a new interest, whether it's handball or ballet or finger painting, I take great delight in arranging an appropriate place for her to pursue that interest. When Nanette or I develop a new enthusiasm, from bread baking to river rafting, part of the fun for me is figuring out how to fit that activity into our existing home and life.

I have been known to design my own furniture, refit existing furniture, move flowerbeds, replace flooring, and constantly rearrange the paintings on the walls in an endless search for the perfect placement of each piece. My artist's obsession with dramatic viewpoints has led me to customize every home I've lived in to maximize the view. In one case, years ago, I even had a small second-story deck reinforced and hired a crane to drop a hot tub into place—the perfect family vantage point for studying the lighting effects in the valley below while soaking in bubbly warm water!

My ongoing efforts to design the perfect workspace for my art—the right easel, the perfect palette, a specialized place for my often homemade tools and supplies—is legendary in our family. It is a quest I started as a teenager, with an old desk that I fitted out and tucked under a loft in my bedroom. And it is a quest I continue today as well. Though I consider my current homemade wooden easel close to perfect, with its counterbalanced canvas rack and heavy-duty construction, I figure there's always room for improvement—and I love the process of tinkering with it.

In addition to shaping our physical space, I take great pleasure in working with Nanette to shape our family's memories. We love to plan unfor-gettable road trips and smaller adventures as well, such as a hike in the woods or a bike ride to the village candy store. (The promise of a sack of sweets can keep even a complaining child pedaling.) We set aside special nights to play games. We try to make the children's homework a family event. The kids help out (sometimes willingly) with household chores, we fit in times of play as much as possible, and we even record the memories we're making with cameras, journals, and an occasional sketchpad. In the process, we are shaping a home that is unique to us, as individual as a fingerprint.

Nanette and I also place high priority on maintaining our relationship with one another and with each of our children. We make time to talk when things are bothering us. We try to negotiate our differences. We do our best to set aside daily "husband and wife" time just to keep in touch. If something isn't working in our life together, we are committed to doing what we can to fix it.

Note that I didn't say "doing what we can to improve the other person." Attempting to change other people is not only an invitation to frustration; it also encourages an attitude of pride. The belief that "I'm right and everyone else is wrong" is inherently counterproductive. It is the very antithesis of loving and cherishing the rooms and relationships that make up a home.

But personalizing a home, adjusting its floor plan or its furnishings or its atmosphere or its daily schedule to suit a family's unique needs—that is quite a different thing. In my experience, the very process of personalizing helps the hearth fires of home burn brighter.

One of the simplest ways I have found to shape the atmosphere of our

home is to adjust the lighting. My interest in lighting, in fact, has become almost an inside joke in our family. I am constantly in the process of dimming the lights or brightening them, turning on lamps and turning them off, opening or closing blinds, lighting candles on the tables or fires in the fireplace — quite literally stoking the home fires. As official "lighting director" of the Kinkade family, I take seriously the cozy effects of lighting that do so much to maintain a family mood.

Another way we personalize our home is by setting up special little corners for activities we like. In our house, these centers tend to come and go as the children's interests change; for instance, a jigsaw puzzle on a table may evolve into a basket full of musical instruments or a guinea pig cage. Because I love to read, I have set up a small reading center in our family room, an easy chair with a good light and a basket beside it for books. And because Nanette likes to keep the children with her while she works in her home office, we have set up a child-sized worktable right next to her big one.

Surrounding ourselves with reminders of who we are and where we've been is another simple way we have found to make our home uniquely ours. The walls, shelves, floors, and windowsills of both our home and my studio are full of objects that tell the stories of where we've been and what we've done and enjoyed together. I've put on proud display a number of personal artifacts that remind me of earlier times in my life — the secondhand easel I bought in art school, for instance, and an old mug that was part of our home when I was growing up (it now holds brushes). Even my hat rack displays an artifact, the battered felt hat that I wore the summer I rode the rails as a hobo.

Even more evocative, to both Nanette and me, is the painting that hangs in our bedroom. It is a nocturne that depicts a teenage boy and girl walking together in the moonlight. I went home and painted it the night after our very first date, when we were still in high school. Years later I showed it to Nanette. Today that reminder of our young love is a precious part of our home, a piece of personal history that brightens our lives when we look at it.

WE ALWAYS DO IT THIS WAY!

One of the most meaningful ways we have found to shape our home and make it uniquely ours is to establish and uphold family rituals. We have found that these deliberately repeated experiences are especially effective ways of building a shared history and nurturing our family relationships. The children, with their inherent love of repetition, thrive on ritual—they love the comfort and security of knowing that "we always" read before going to bed or "we always" pile together on Mom and Dad's bed on Saturday morning.

Some of our most meaningful family rituals center around dinnertime, which for us is family conversation time. By choice and now by tradition, we turn off the radio, set aside toys and reading matter, and refuse to answer the phone. We gather around the table at the same time each day, hold hands and say a simple blessing, pass around the food. And then we talk. We share our days. We tell each other jokes. We try to practice our manners—and we're all getting better! This time of quiet sharing (with occasional protests over having to eat vegetables) has become very important to all of us, and we try not to miss it when we're home.

We've recently set up another ritual very deliberately as a way to help our older daughters know their grandmother better. My mother recently moved to be near us, and the centerpiece of her home is a stately old piano. Our two oldest girls have been taking piano lessons for some time now. Three or four times a week, therefore, we send our daughters one at a time over to Grandma's house to practice. So far the combination of regular visits and regular practice is paying enormous benefits both in terms of music and our family relationships.

Nanette and I, too, have come to appreciate the home-building quality of ritual in our life. Our evening cup of peppermint tea together serves that purpose for us. It gives us the opportunity to relax and "debrief" at the end of the day, enjoying each other's company as well as the warmth and fragrance of peppermint. Our daily exercise time is another ritual that helps keep the hearth fires of our relationship burning warmly. Rather than heading to a local gymnasium as a means to stay fit, we instead take a brisk daily walk together, rain or shine.

Whenever we can, in fact, we try to light some literal hearthfires, for gathering around the fire is another thing we "always do" as a family. We love to snuggle together in front of the family room fireplace. Even better are the times we light a campfire in the brick firepit outside. This outdoor campsite is a new discovery at our house; we had thought it was a planter until we accidentally discovered the gas pipes leading into it. Now we have a place right at home where we can toast marshmallows, sing camp songs, and tell stories out under the stars. In the process we are growing closer with every shared experience.

I can't wait for the day when I overhear my girls tell their children that "we always" gathered around the campfire together when they were small — making ourselves ever more comfortable and joyful through the rituals that make our house a home.

Rituals encase memories. They link the past and present.
They choreograph the dance of intimacy that families and friends perform.
They give us access to one another.
— WENDY M. WRIGHT

OUT FROM THE CENTER

The principles of making yourself at home must start with your inner circle, with your actual dwelling and the people who share it. But the warmth of this kind of "homemaking" quickly spreads out from the center to warm the widening circles of neighborhood and community, friends and colleagues, all the places and relationships that define where you belong. These, too, are to be cherished. And these, too, though to a lesser extent, can be shaped to suit who you are and what you need.

At our particular season of home life, Nanette and I have chosen to confine most of our "homemaking" to our inner circle. Because my work life is somewhat public, our lives very busy, and our children still quite small, we focus primarily on loving each other, attending to one another's comforts and needs, supporting one another. We protect our family time, and this means we limit the time we spend with others. What little outside involvement we do have tends to be with extended family and very close friends.

At the same time, we are well aware that no man (or family!) is an island. We know our neighbors and speak to them regularly. We take walks on the neighborhood streets and visit the town parks. We involve ourselves in church activities. We invite people over for dinner, and we socialize with business acquaintances, though less frequently than some would consider standard. Nanette often invites our children's friends over to play, and from

time to time we'll bring a little guest along on family adventures.

And we do foresee a time, perhaps when the children are older, when the walls surrounding our inner circle will grow a bit more permeable. As our children grow, we would like for our home to be a homey, comfortable gathering place for their friends. We may socialize more with our friends as well and perhaps become more involved in community activities.

Your circumstances, however, may be different, and these differences will affect the degree of your involvement with the home outside your walls. If you live alone, as my mother does, you may have to look outside your dwelling for companionship. If you are new in a community, like my friend Anne and her family, you will need to expend some of your energy to make friends and even to find your way around. You may even decide, like certain wonderful people I have known, that sharing your house and your life with those outside your inner circle is part of the focus of your life, something you are called to do.

How do you know that it's time to widen the circles of involvement and reach out beyond the walls to make yourself at home? If you don't know your neighbors, that's a sign. If you are not involved in at least one set of outside activities, or if no one else ever visits you, that's another indicator. If you feel a kind of inner tug that tells you it's time to expand your world, it might be time to pay attention.

The best thing to do after that is to take small steps to expand the walls of your world.

First, look at the world immediately outside your door, your neighborhood. It may consist of the other apartments in your complex, the other houses on your block, or the other farm along your rural route. But you can make yourself at home with your neighbors as you begin the process of cherishing your shared environment, building a history together, and nurturing the network of your relationships.

Start by simply taking a walk. Take a walk every day and nod or smile at the people you see regularly. From this simple base of familiarity, reach out a little further. You can take a pie to a new neighbor or invite another neighbor over for tea. You can offer a cutting from your garden to the woman next door or volunteer to bring in another neighbor's paper while he is out of

town. Even better, you can organize a committee to throw a neighborhood event—a block party or even a Fourth of July parade.

Beyond your neighborhood, the principles for making yourself at home in your workplace and your community are the same. At work, you have a ready-made group of potential friends, men and women who already share a history with you. Although socializing with colleagues—true socializing, as opposed to business meetings or business functions—will depend on your circumstances, it almost never hurts to reach out to a coworker by helping him or her in the photocopy room or asking that person to lunch.

For Nanette and me, our church has been our family outside our family for many years. We have come to depend on the help and prayers of our brothers and sisters there, and so we highly recommend making yourself at home in the wider circles of your life by becoming involved with a center of religious worship and fellowship. Even if you have no interest in organized religion, however, you may find a similar home outside your home in a community organization, a volunteer agency, or an interest group such as a reading club or sports team. Look for people who share your interests, and look for an opportunity to work together as well as socialize. The sharing of a task tends to build stronger bonds of friendship and connection than almost any other activity.

ALWAYS AT HOME

In all your efforts to make yourself at home in the wider circles of your community, remember the principles that will help the hearth fires glow brighter.

Remember to cherish your home—within or without your walls—as well as to live there. Stop from time to time and gaze around and appreciate what you see. Make the conscious decision to love the place where you live and the people you live with—even if, at the moment, that act of love requires all your imagination.

Remember, also, to be yourself and to surround yourself with people and things that both define and reflect who you are. If you love red zinnias, plant your gardens with red zinnias. If you love clowns (as a former landlady of mine did), fill your home with stuffed clowns, porcelain clowns, clown paintings. Better yet, dress up as a clown from time to time and visit the children's ward of a hospital, or join a group that does so on a regular basis. Don't be afraid to expend the time and energy to bring the world of your home closer to being your ideal world.

And remember, most of all, to be thankful that you have a place on this earth — a physical spot to call your home, a history that tells your story, a nest of relationships that make you who you are.

A glowing hearth is a choice you make, but it's also a wonderful gift.

Celebrate it. Enjoy it. Stoke the hearth fires and stir up the flames of love and joy.

Every day of your life on this earth, the choices you make can keep you constantly anchored to a stable, warm center.

Your home, the place where love and joy and tranquillity burn the brightest.

My joy burns brighter
when I tend to the glowing hearth fires of home.

LIGHTPOSTS
FOR LIVING

EIGHT

A SERVANT'S HEART

LIVING IN A SELFLESS LIGHT

*A little Consideration, a little Thought for Others,
makes all the difference.*
— EEYORE THE DONKEY

I'll never forget the day when the lights came on in my life.

I was sitting in an art class at the University of California at Berkeley, listening to yet another erudite professor ramble on about the nature and purpose of art. The gist of the lecture was that the artist is by definition on the fringes of society and is responsible only to the demands of a personal artistic vision. Art exists for itself alone. It is in essence a private language whose sole purpose is to allow the artist to express himself.

"Your art is all about you," the professor droned. "It doesn't matter if anyone else appreciates it. It doesn't matter if anyone else enjoys it. It doesn't even matter if anyone else understands it. All that is important is you." And so on, and so forth.

I had heard it all before. To be honest, it more or less underscored my attitude about my own art at that time. Although even then my artistic interests and subjects differed from those of many of my classmates, my essential motivation *was* self-expression. I painted what I liked, because I liked to do it. I had never really questioned this fundamental artistic motivation—until now.

Now for the first time, as I sat in that class listening to the ideas I had heard a million times, I felt something deep inside me rebel.

If my art is only about me, I wondered, *if it speaks only in an esoteric language that no one else can understand, what's the point?*

Suddenly I realized that the self-centered, self-serving artistic approach I was being taught was just the opposite of what I wanted my life and my art to be about. And at that moment a different philosophy began to form itself in my mind, one that has driven my life and career ever since.

My art, I realized, is not about me; it's about you. I paint because the act of creation brings me pleasure, but I also paint to benefit and enrich the life experience of others.

I realized that my life and my talent are gifts, and they have been given to me for the purpose of helping others. So what I wanted to do as a painter was not just to express myself, but to create pictures that encouraged people, that brought them a sense of peace and joy, that inspired them to catch a vision for a better life. I wanted to create pictures that people from all backgrounds could understand and appreciate, that spoke a universal language of beauty and serenity. I wanted, through my art and through my life, to make somebody else's life a little better and brighter.

But then I wondered: Can an artist really make a difference in someone else's life through painting pictures? If I wanted to help others, perhaps I should give up my art studies and become a doctor or a teacher. Perhaps I should work with the poor in a ghetto or move to the African bush and become a missionary.

I honestly didn't know if an artist could make a difference or not. But because I felt such a strong calling to paint (and not the slightest sense of being equipped to go to Africa), I decided to go ahead with the experiment. I would attempt to be a painter with a servant's heart, one whose life and work and talents were committed to the service of others.

Gradually, over the years, as I continued examining my philosophy of blessing others through my work, I began to see the miracle unfolding. When I painted with the purpose of giving, when I kept my heart open to other people and their needs as I worked, people *did* receive a blessing from my art. They told me so. I saw it in their eyes. And then, as the joy of serving began to fill my heart, I began to look for other ways I could use my art to serve others.

That is when the idea of publishing my art began. I didn't want to produce paintings only for the people who could afford originals. I wanted to make art of the highest quality I could create, but also make it affordable to people in many income brackets. I knew I couldn't produce paintings for everybody; there simply aren't enough hours in the day. So Nanette and I started a company that would publish my work in many other forms—as limited-edition fine-art prints on canvas and paper, as calendars, as note cards, in books.

Today, the many letters we receive on a yearly basis are evidence that this approach to serving others through my painting has made a positive impact on the lives of at least some people. I know this is true because people rarely comment on the technical aspect of my work. They don't write me with analyses of my use of color and composition or to praise my brushwork. Instead, they give me testimonies about the peace of mind a particular painting brought them, the hope they feel when they look at a certain image. They say they have been reminded through my work that there are still good things in this world, that tranquillity and beauty are still available.

How touching and inspiring these testimonials are to me! During the many years that have passed since the light came on in my mind during that college art class, I have gradually begun to see my paintings being used to touch the lives of others. Any questions I once had about how a painter could be of service have been laid to rest. I know I'm far from being a saint, but I believe I have made a difference. And it all began with a simple desire to serve, to be available, to use my energies and my talents and my time to make someone else's life a little better.

"That man," said the little prince to himself,
". . . is the only one of them all who does not seem to me ridiculous.
Perhaps that is because he is thinking of something else besides himself."
—ANTOINE DE SAINT-EXUPÉRY

THE BIG INSIGHT

My mother told me not long ago about a televised interview she saw in which a famous actor was being quizzed about his movies, his family life, and especially his work on behalf of the underprivileged in Third World countries. The interviewer gushed, in typical Hollywood fashion: "I'm such an admirer of yours—you seem so together! What's your secret?"

"Well," he answered, "about five years ago I had the Big Insight. And this was it: *What I do for others is more important than what I do for myself.*"

That phrase has stuck with me since the day I heard it because it echoes my own experience—and because I believe it holds an absolutely essential key to a life that shines with joy. Although it runs counter to the dominant messages of our self-centered culture and the habits of our self-centered nature, it taps deep into a paradoxical principle of life that has been observed throughout the centuries, in every culture.

This is it: When it comes to deep, lasting happiness, self-serving just isn't what it's cracked up to be. Those who live only for themselves will be stuck with themselves—and little else. Those who give of themselves, on the other hand, move closer and closer to discovering the secrets of lasting joy.

This principle, I have come to believe, is stitched deep in the fabric of the universe. It's one of the basic laws of creation: The flow of blessings in our life is directly related to our passing blessings along to someone else.

But let's face it: This principle of giving and receiving may be a basic law of creation, but we're not born knowing it! As a matter of fact, we come into this world taking, grasping, clinging tight. We have to *learn* to give, *learn* to share, *learn* to think of others. We have to learn to hold life loosely and freely—to give away our time and energy and money for the purpose of helping others, trusting that there will still be enough to take care of our needs and give us joy. We need to learn to trust the counterintuitive reality that unclenching our fists and opening our hands to give will enable us also to catch the blessings that come our way. Most of us have to learn this truth again and again before we completely believe it.

☀

Tuning Your Heart

So how do you learn to trust the Big Insight? How do you learn to make selflessness a guiding principle in your life?

If you are like most people, you want your life to amount to something. You want a happy life, and you also have a deep desire to make a difference. You may have already had your version of the Big Insight and are looking for better ways to serve and bless others. Or you may simply feel dissatisfied with the joy level in your life and are looking for a different, more fulfilling approach to living.

In either case, the way to start is to make a simple decision that service to others will be a priority in your life. If you keep a list of goals, pencil in an additional item that has to do with helping others. If such an item is already there, pencil in a check mark beside it and get to work. Make a list of possibilities and check them off: Pay a compliment to a colleague. Say yes to the neighbor's request for help. Volunteer for a few hours at the animal shelter.

What I wouldn't recommend, at least not at first, is making any kind of big change in your life. Don't quit your job and move to the ghetto to work with abandoned children, at least not yet. Don't give away your savings to charitable causes, at least not right away.

Instead, focus on one simple question: What small things can I do today to bring a blessing to someone else?

In my experience, the initial urge to make a grand gesture or a major sacrifice is usually more selfish than selfless. It is more likely to arise out of the desire to be seen as a hero or to impress others rather than out of a true desire to serve. While such an act may be its own reward—it may well bring you attention or admiration—it won't bring the true blessing that comes from acting on behalf of others.

There's another reason, as well. Bringing blessings to others is in essence a habit, a daily way of life. And habits, by nature, grow out of repetition—by countless small, daily acts repeated often enough to feel like second nature. You may continue doing the same things you do every day—the same job, the same family involvements, the same leisure activities—but in all these things you will be looking for ways to make other people's lives better.

When you work, for instance, you can bless others by treating your boss or your employees with respect. You nod and smile at other people in the hall-ways, even if you're feeling stressed. You compliment the delivery person on her efficiency. (I have found that a simple compliment can be a profound blessing.) You go the second mile on a project and even offer to help a colleague with a project that is overwhelming her. You remember to clean out the cof-feepot in the break room.

On the way home, when the homeless person on the corner gives his usual request for a handout, perhaps you give him one. Better yet, if you have time, perhaps you take him into a nearby café and order him dinner.

Then, at home, you resist the urge to leave your heart of service at the door. (Strangely enough, blessing the people you love on a daily basis can be the most challenging act of service you encounter!) Instead of plunking down in front of the TV, you help your son with his homework. When your little daughter asks the same question for the fifteenth time, you try to answer it patiently. You give your spouse a back rub. Just for tonight, you do the household chores carefully and without complaining.

And no, you won't manage all this every day. Some days you'll feel and act selfish and grouchy. Other days, you'll do selfless things for selfish motives. This is because you're human. But the good news is that humans are also capable of giving, sharing, blessing—and that's the direction you're heading. Through repeated small acts of kindness, of thoughtfulness, of bless-ing, you will gradually be tuning your heart to play a different melody.

There's more than one way, you see, to tune a musical instrument such as a guitar (or so my musical friends tell me). By tightening the strings bit by bit, you adjust the notes that the strings will play. In the process, you change the way the whole instrument sounds. The fingering may be the same. The instrument is the same. But if the strings are tuned differently, the sound will be different.

And that's exactly what you're working toward as you practice acts of everyday service. For each successful act of daily blessing you manage, in fact, you'll find that your heartstrings are tugged another notch toward being tuned for service. You'll begin to realize the rewards that come from blessing others—the smiles of appreciation from people at work, the thanks from the homeless person, the joy and enthusiasm of your children, the sighs of plea-sure from your spouse as you rub his or her neck.

Even if your coworkers are surly and the homeless person is unappreciative and your children are unruly and your spouse has too much on his or her mind to pay attention to you, you'll probably find a sense of satisfaction just from attempting to be of service. Your joy will begin to build, and you'll be motivated to attempt more acts of service. Before long you'll notice that your fists have unclenched, your shoulders have relaxed, the worry lines in your brow have smoothed a bit, and your heart is humming in the incomparable key of joy.

JOIN THE RANDOM KINDNESS MOVEMENT

One of the most joyful and fun things you can do to tune your heart toward service is to take the advice of the bumper stickers and "practice random acts of kindness and senseless acts of beauty." A woman named Anne Herbert coined that phrase in 1982; she scrawled it onto a placemat of a Sausalito, California, restaurant. Something about that little phrase, with its quiet challenge to the random and senseless violence in our society, caught the imagination of the public. A book by the same name suggested some great ideas—then spawned several sequels. Schools and other organizations began stressing the idea, and now there's even a Random Act of Kindness Day (February 17).

What exactly is a random act of kindness? They're similar to the daily acts of blessing I've described, but with a more spontaneous, extravagant flavor. In the foreword to the book *Random Acts of Kindness*, Daphne Rose Kingma describes them as "those little sweet or grand lovely things we do for no reason except that, momentarily, the best of our humanity has sprung, exquisitely, into full bloom . . . you are doing not what life requires of you, but what the best of your human soul invites you to do."

Random acts don't require any strategic planning or long-term commitment. They don't require large amounts of money or time. They raise few questions as to long-term consequences or ongoing expectations. All they do require is the ability to notice another person and perform a single, creative act for that person's benefit. And the benefits they pay are quite disproportional in terms of satisfaction. There's a built-in sense of fun and mischief; you almost feel like you've gotten away with something wonderful. Usually you can't wait to do it again.

The books that furthered this movement (including *Random Acts of Kindness* and *Kids' Random Acts of Kindness*) are full of ideas you might want to try, but it's not hard to invent your own. It may be as simple as moving a newspaper from a neighbor's front lawn onto the porch. It may be as romantic as picking up the tab for the young couple at the next table who are obviously splurging on a nice restaurant meal. It may be as practical as picking up litter in the park or as quirky as giving away your umbrella in a downpour. The amount of money or time you spend is up to you. The point is to make a gesture just for the sake of being nice.

One woman I read about, who lives in a cold climate, made a game of getting to the parking lot first after work and scraping the ice and snow off her coworkers' windows. Another gentleman, after he finished edging his lawn, took his edger over and did his neighbor's lawn as well. People have paid tolls for others, slipped quarters into expired parking meters, tucked ten-dollar bills into purses and wallets. Our own family has been known to buy a bag of oranges in a big city and go down the street sharing them with less fortunate people we meet.

The possibilities are endless. The joy-dividends are enormous. Best of all, random acts of kindness are both habit-forming and contagious. One kind act seems to call for another, and everyone benefits. The fun and satisfaction you derive from your "random acts of kindness and senseless acts of beauty" will be a source of inspiration and motivation in the process of developing a servant's heart.

*I think there were not in all the city four merrier people
than the hungry little girls who gave away their breakfasts and
contented themselves with bread and milk on Christmas morning.
"That's loving our neighbor better than ourselves, and I like it," said Meg.*
—LOUISA MAY ALCOTT

WHAT'S YOUR CALLING?

The acts of blessing I have described thus far are acts that anyone can (and should) do. They involve no big commitment of time or money or energy, no change in life direction. Their very beauty lies in the fact that they are done "on the side," as it were, in the course of doing your job, pursuing your hobbies, and just living life.

But if such small deeds of thoughtful kindness can provide such enormous benefits, consider the joy-rewards that come from focusing your giving into a conscious, long-term commitment. Think of this as your special calling, the form of long-term service that is especially suited to your interests and talents, the place where you can serve the world best by concentrating your time and your energy. I believe that every person at any given time is gifted with such a calling, and finding and following it may well be the most important mission of your life.

How do you know what these best areas of service are? The process of discerning your calling requires looking and listening, but it's not necessarily a matter of hearkening to a loud voice from heaven. In my own experience, at least, the answer can often be found by thoughtfully (and prayerfully) answering these questions:

First, ask yourself, *What pulls at my heart?* What kinds of needs do you encounter that bring a lump to your throat or an indignant thought of "Somebody oughta do something!" What kinds of situations tend to interest you or concern you? If the picture of a neglected puppy in the newspaper or the skinny kitten nosing in a garbage can brings a tear to your eye, perhaps your call lies along the lines of helping animals. If you find yourself angry at stories of financial mismanagement of charitable agencies, perhaps you are being called to volunteer your own financial expertise or administrative talents.

This process of discerning your true and most important call can be tricky. Needs are all around you, and if you have a tender heart, many are likely to draw your attention. As you attempt to sort these out, you might find another question helpful: *What specific needs can be met only by me?* Are there duties that, if you don't attend to them, something unique to the world might be lost? They might be the best place to begin focusing your servant's heart.

You might not be accustomed to thinking of your unique contribution to the world. But I believe to the depths of my being that you have one. Somewhere out there is a unique place for you to serve, a unique life role for you to fill. Only you can make your particular contribution to humankind.

Perhaps only you, with your background in Asian languages, your talent for teaching, and your gift for organization, are uniquely qualified to administer the English as a Second Language program at your local high school. Perhaps you're the only one who cares deeply enough about the litter around the lake near you to organize a cleanup campaign. Whatever your call or circumstances, the "only I" criterion can help you narrow the focus of your efforts, at least at first.

I do think it's perfectly legitimate to ask, *What do I like to do? What do I do well? What brings me joy? How can my current vocation or avocation be used as a tool for passing along blessings for others?* As I have indicated, your current job or hobby may also offer your own best opportunity for service. Almost any job or activity can be undertaken with a view toward service or blessing, and I think it's a mistake to assume that we are serving only when we are doing something we don't enjoy.

You may already be involved in circumstances that give you your greatest opportunity for serving others. If you think this is true, all you have to do is renew your commitment to serve others through what you do and go about your efforts with a servant's heart, a cheerful spirit, and a commitment to true excellence.

If cooking is your primary passion, for instance, it just makes sense for you to bless others by serving them dinner, taking them pies, even planning the menus for Meals on Wheels. If horses are your life, there's no reason you can't share your love by offering rides to underprivileged kids or fostering an animal that has been abused.

You probably don't need to sacrifice who you are, in other words, to receive the blessings of your calling. More likely, in the process of serving others, you'll discover the ultimate fulfillment of who you are—and who you can be.

I have certainly found this to be true in my life. My two chief priorities, my family and my art, are also, I believe, the chief areas where I am called to serve, at least at present. In my work as a painter, I try to encourage people and inspire them with a vision of a more joyful world. In my work as a father, my goal is to raise secure, unselfish children who contribute to making the world a better place. Whether I succeed in these endeavors is another issue. They are still the paths of service that draw my heart most powerfully. I truly believe I am called not only to serve my work and my family, but also to serve others *through* my work and through my family.

I find that keeping these two service priorities first in my mind helps tremendously in my decisions about other areas in which I am asked to serve. It's a simple fact that one person cannot do everything. I don't believe that one person is *supposed* to do everything. The world is full of needs, and we each have unique ways we can contribute to helping meet those needs.

I am not talking about taking the easy way out. I'm certainly not talking about just taking on "fun" projects or doing only what we like to do. Service by definition includes a certain amount of personal sacrifice, and most acts of service include at least some elements that are tiresome or inconvenient or even painful.

I am talking about efficiency in giving—making the best use of our available time and energy by concentrating our efforts in the areas where we are called. Often, I believe, we make the best contribution in areas where our hearts call us to serve—and often these are areas where we have either a natural talent or an interest.

At this time, for instance, I honestly don't believe I am called to run a soup kitchen in the ghetto. I may contribute financially to such a worthy cause and even volunteer to work there occasionally, perhaps as a holiday activity with my family. But because I don't believe I am called to concentrate my energies in these areas, I would feel no guilt in saying no if I was asked to make a major investment of my time in a local soup kitchen.

Similarly, although my Christian faith is extremely important to me, I don't believe I am called to be a preacher or an evangelist. Although I enjoy talking about my art, my calling is not that of a teacher or speaker. I have no difficulty, therefore, in turning down offers for workshops and speaking engagements. And yet I might well say yes to a request to help with the local children's art center, a form of service that dovetails with my chosen avenues of service.

Over time, of course, all this may change. When my children are older, for instance, I may find it's time to involve myself more fully in some form of hands-on volunteer work. I may find a new passion emerging in my heart to speak at conferences or to serve on the board of some charitable organization.

And this may well be true for you as well, either now or later. Even as you make the effort to bless others through what you are called to do on a daily basis, you may gradually discern the call to something quite different, something that could determine the course of your future life. Perhaps you work in accounting but are beginning to think about pursuing a teaching degree. Perhaps you work in an advertising office during the day, but get your best sense of satisfaction through the volunteer work you do at a local retirement center. These inklings, these little stirrings or dissatisfactions, deserve your careful thought and prayers, for they may well indicate a call to move toward a different area of service.

DON'T DEPEND ON THE RESULTS

Developing a servant's heart can be one of the most satisfying undertakings of your life. The more you learn to focus on blessing others, the more freely the blessings will flow in your life. At the same time, you would do well

to keep a few things in mind that can help you avoid disappointment.

First of all, although you can expect a blessing from serving others, you can't always expect to see *results*.

You may help a homeless person get to a doctor, but you may not be able to ensure that he takes his medication. You may not be able to keep him from sliding deeper into the web of problems that put him on the street. He may not even appreciate your efforts or say thank you. You may never see him again.

It's a pitfall, in other words, to engage in acts of blessing or charity with the expectation of a specific reward. Neat, warm, fuzzy endings are the stuff of motion pictures, not necessarily of real life. The truth is that you may never know the outcome of a particular act of service or you may not see results for many years. The blessing you *can* expect is the satisfaction of serving, the sense of being connected with others, of doing a good thing.

I believe, as well, that you can expect good things to happen to you that are seemingly unrelated to your acts of goodness toward others. This is a hard concept to pin down. It's hard to prove, but I have seen it happen repeatedly in my own life. The more I do for others, the more good things seem to happen to me. I may not receive a thank-you from a down-and-outer I took to the doctor, but I may have someone stop to help when my battery goes dead in the grocery store parking lot. When it comes to service, to paraphrase the Bible, "As you plant, so shall you reap." But the harvest doesn't always come in the form that you expect. That means you are better off, in the long run, to put your expectations on hold and concentrate on finding joy in the act of service itself.

TAKE CARE OF YOURSELF

Here's another crucial thing to keep in mind when it comes to service: You will do it better if you take care of yourself. Serving others, in other words, does not mean sacrificing all your own needs. It doesn't mean giving up everything you like to do. In my experience, in fact, those who continually neglect their own needs in the interest of serving others can often become self-pitying martyrs instead of joyful servants. They are also more susceptible to cynicism, bitterness, and burnout than those who accept their human limitations and do what is necessary to refresh their minds and souls and bodies.

There are times—in fact, there are many times—when the call of service means putting someone else's needs above our own. Certainly there are times

when you'll have to face down your own selfishness and inertia and do something you just don't feel like doing at the moment. You'll choose to read to your child although you really would like to collapse on the couch. Or you'll help renovate an elderly friend's house even though the thought of pounding nails in the hot sun doesn't sound like your idea of fun. You'll follow up with service commitments you made, even those that have come to be inconvenient.

Choosing to put another's needs above your own, however, doesn't mean ignoring your own needs for rest, for refreshment, for nourishment. To lead an effective life of service, you really do need to take care of yourself.

If someone were to ask me what is the most difficult lesson I've learned from
[being paralyzed], I'm very clear about it:
I know I have to give when sometimes I really want to take.
— CHRISTOPHER REEVE

On the most basic level, this means paying attention to what your body needs to function properly. You don't really serve more effectively when you are improperly nourished, inadequately exercised, and chronically sleep-deprived. Your service is not more valuable when it stresses you out. If anything, you can devote more energy to the service of others when you set aside time to keep your body healthy.

The same applies to your need for emotional and mental refreshment. If you truly want to bless others in your life, you must seek out those experiences that keep you motivated and inspired.

If you are the type who needs time alone to recharge your batteries, for instance, it's up to you to guard your alone time. Take advantage of nearby retreat centers on a regular basis, or just find a quiet corner of a local park.

If, on the other hand, you are a more gregarious sort who picks up energy and inspiration from other people, look for partners in service. Try joining a charitable organization where you can bless others as part of a team. Or ask several friends to join you in a particular act of service.

Don't forget to seek out the daily perks and joyful surprises that your life has to offer. Even as you look for opportunities to serve, look as well for opportunities to enjoy. Savoring the moments of every day and enjoying the blessings of your own life will not make you more selfish. If anything, they will make you more caring. We give most willingly out of gratitude, out of a sense of our own abundance. The more you let yourself feel blessed, the more you'll feel the motivation to bless others.

Serving may feel like a sacrifice at times, but you really don't need to sacrifice who you are and what you need to receive the blessings of service. You just need to learn to relax, to open up your hands, to let God's laws of blessing operate the way they were designed to do.

Then the abundance will begin to flow from your servant's heart to the heart of others . . . and back again.

The Big Insight is eternally true:
The more I give myself to others,
the more joy and inner peace will flow into my own life.

LIGHTPOSTS
FOR LIVING

NINE

SAYING GRACE

LIVING IN THE LIGHT OF THANKFULNESS

I can no other answer make but thanks . . . and ever thanks.
— WILLIAM SHAKESPEARE

Remember when it was fun to look at the world through color-tinted glasses—or any kind of glasses at all?

As a boy, I was fascinated to discover that everything around me looked different when viewed through different lenses. I loved to peer through Grandma's thick-lensed bifocals at a world gone fuzzy and strange. (How could she see through those?) I delighted in sunglasses that darkened my vision or those little paper spectacles that popped movies into 3-D relief. Best of all were the cheap "prism" glasses from a cereal box that seemed to paint little rainbows around the edges of everything, even my sneakers and the dog and the dirty laundry.

I learned early, therefore, that how you see the world depends to a great extent on what lens you're looking through.

And here's something else I learned that, to a great extent, has colored the rest of my life: My whole life seems to take on a rosy glow when viewed through the lens of gratitude.

The older I grow, in fact, the more I suspect that the amount of joy in my heart is directly related to the thankfulness in my attitude. When I think of the past with gratitude, even my painful memories are softened by a realization that I have survived and learned. When I think of the present with gratitude, my natural impulse is to live in the moment and enjoy it. When I look toward the future with gratitude, I expect tomorrow to be filled with wonderful discoveries and growth, just as yesterday and today have been.

Gratitude is not precisely the same thing as optimism. It's more the attitude that makes optimism possible. It is essentially a habit of thinking, a way of understanding who we are and what happens in our lives. That means, of course, that looking at life through the lens of gratitude is something each of us can do. We can choose gratitude. And here is the fundamental conviction that we must engrave on our hearts if we want the rosy glow of gratitude to light up our lives: Life is a gift, a wonderful, stupendous, miraculous gift. It's not something we deserve or purchase with our efforts. It is simply there for us every morning, waiting for us to unwrap and enjoy. Every moment, in fact, we have the opportunity to open another tiny package in the gift of our days.

Often we unwrap a delightful surprise—a hug from a child, an afternoon under blue skies, a successful attempt at something new. Other times, we pull at the wrappings to discover a painful experience—a snub from an acquaintance, an argument with a spouse, a humiliating failure. Sometimes the experience in the box is just disappointingly dull. But unwrapping even these mundane life-gifts can be a little like finding a kitchen appliance or a ratchet set under the Christmas tree. They are tools to teach us or help us grow, and the joy we discover in them depends on understanding their usefulness.

All of life, even the painful or dull moments, is a gift. That's the place to start if you want to learn to look through the rosy lens of gratitude.

THANKFULNESS—WHAT'S IN IT FOR YOU?

If you're like me, you probably had certain habits of thankfulness drilled into you as a child. You're supposed to say thank you when receiving a treat, and you're supposed to write a thank-you note for a gift or visit. I wonder, though, if anyone ever bothered to make it clear to you what thankfulness can do for you as an attitude, a basic way of looking at life—how, specifically, it can bring you joy.

In the first place, thankfulness can reduce stress in your life by making you more content with who you are and what you have. If you make a habit of accepting every circumstance gratefully and assuming there is a purpose in it, you'll be relieved from the worry and anxiety that go with being resentful and dissatisfied. If you can approach every experience as a gift, even if it's not exactly what you had in mind, you can just say thank you and go on with your life instead of stewing over what you think you were entitled to.

Say, for example, that you're working hard on an office deadline, putting in a lot of overtime, and you come down with the flu. You can barely lift your head off the pillow, let alone drive to your office and work. By the time you return to the land of the living, the deadline is long past, and your project is a lost cause.

If you look upon this circumstance as an undeserved calamity, you'll probably end up obsessing over why such a thing had to happen to you, how horrible you feel, and what else could go wrong. But what if you insist on thinking of even this illness as a gift, assuming it has a purpose? If you can accept it with even reluctant thanks, you'll probably begin seeing the ways that this miserable bout with the flu can be of help. Perhaps it's a sign that you need to take better care of yourself. Perhaps you wouldn't have made the deadline anyway and your illness has protected you from embarrassment. Perhaps your spouse really pitched in to nurse you back to health and your relationship was in some way deepened. The very act of realizing these advantages can help your worry and tension begin to drain away. It might even help you recover faster.

An attitude of thankfulness can also increase your joy by increasing your sense of abundant blessing. When you deliberately focus your attention on the blessings in your life and receive them gratefully, you gradually develop a clearer sense of just how much there is to be thankful for. This is the exact point of the old practice of "counting blessings." Often it's only when you start counting that you realize how many you really have.

It's like having a warehouse stuffed with both trash and treasure. It's hard to see through all that clutter to know just what you have. But if you gather all the treasure together in one place, you suddenly realize you have enough to fill several floors—and that's when you feel rich beyond measure.

The third way thankfulness can add to your joy is a little trickier to understand. Thankfulness helps you maintain an accurate perspective on just who you are and what you deserve. Gratitude, in other words, is the antidote to pride, which is the error of judgment that leaves you thinking you are either better or worse than you really are or that you deserve better or worse than you have received. When you insist on viewing life through a lens of gratitude, you move toward a sense of self that is both confident and humble—a truly healthy outlook on life. Your sense of trust increases, and your need to control others diminishes.

That brings us to the fourth and, to me, most important advantage of maintaining a thankful attitude: It builds relationships. It's no accident, you see, that the process of giving and receiving gifts is basic to the social interaction of any culture. When someone responds to a gift with gratitude, both giver and recipient feel more joy, and the ties between them are strengthened. Accordingly, when we make the choice to respond with gratitude to the circumstances of our lives, we see more clearly the contributions made by other people, and the act of expressing our gratitude draws us closer to these people. Even more important, our sense of spiritual connection is strengthened by practicing an attitude of thankfulness for every day and every moment. As a Christian, I find that giving thanks for the gift of life brings me ever closer to the Giver of that life.

※

CELEBRATING THE GIFT OF YOURSELF

Adopting a lens of thankfulness makes your life better. That's just a fact. I've seen it work in enough lives—especially my own—to be certain of that.

At the same time, if you've ever been a child muttering a forced thank-you to a less-than-favorite relative at a family gathering, you know that saying thank you and actually *being* thankful are not always the same thing.

Even with the benefits clear, the fact remains that most of us don't *feel* thankful all the time. So the natural question is: How do you make yourself more thankful?

I think the best way to begin is by celebrating *yourself*.

This doesn't mean adopting a selfish outlook or focusing only on your own needs. It does mean doing everything you can to realize the inherent privilege of waking up every morning as you.

It means, for instance, rejoicing in the fact that you have a body. Regardless of its failings (which you may be all too accustomed to reciting), it still performs its job in wonderful ways. It carries you around, connects you to the world through its senses, and enables you to process the information you

receive. It carries on the basic functions of sustaining life—heartbeat, breathing, digestion—with surprisingly little fuss, especially considering the abuse it sometimes takes. Even if your body differs from the standard model— if, for example, it cannot walk or hear—it still offers you countless options for joy and usefulness.

One of the most delightful things about small children is their absolute fascination with the fact that they have bodies. Watch a baby stare at her toes, watch a five-year-old discover new forms of motion. They're in on the secret. Having a body is a wondrous gift.

Blessings are like hugs from God to let you know how much He loves you.
Counting blessings is like hugging God back.
—DEBBY BOONE

The same thing applies to the mind and spirit that occupy your body. You have been gifted with a unique self, an unprecedented personality, a custom-made set of talents and abilities. No one will ever relate to the world exactly the way you do. That, too, is sound reason for gratitude.

Even the particular set of circumstances that have brought you to this moment of reading are appropriate grounds for thanks. Regardless of what you think of the particular man and woman who conceived you, for instance, they still participated in giving you the opportunity of life and making you the particular person you are. Chances are, they also loved you and did the best they could to raise you.

Even if your parents were less than perfect (whose are?) you can rejoice that they were handpicked out of the billions of people alive on our planet to unite together to form you. I believe in the divine appointment of parents, that they are specially chosen for each individual. With all their failings—and even if they were totally absent from your life—they still played a major part in shaping who you are.

Like many children from a broken home, I used to dream of having parents who were still married. Now I can see that, had I grown up with an active father in the home, I might not have grown to be the somewhat self-reliant and independent person I became. It's taken me some time, but I've come to appreciate that God knew what he was doing when he chose both of my parents for me and allowed the circumstances of my upbringing.

Even if the years behind you were full of pain, the fact remains that someone made it possible for you to survive. Someone taught you to read, to cook, to sing, or to plant flowers. The people who loved you and even those who refused to love you shaped you into what you are today and gave you the tools you need to shape your own tomorrow. That in itself is a reason for gratitude.

Your present circumstances, too, are part of the gift of who you are. Most likely, you have a home, a place where your physical and emotional needs can be met. You probably have a family of some sort, connected to you by bonds of blood or commitment. You have a job, a way of making a living.

And even if you don't have one or the other of these things, you have the ability to move toward a better future. You have possibilities—a gift that is offered only to the living on this earth. So celebrate the fact that you are who you are, where you are—and affirm the inherent goodness of living by saying *thank you.*

TAKING YOURSELF WITH A GRAIN OF SALT

Even as you celebrate the gift of yourself, however, the very act of living with thanksgiving means learning to take yourself with a grain of salt. It means maintaining a healthy perspective about who you are: a mixture of sugar and vinegar, of good and bad, of dazzling wonder and glaring imperfection. It means owning up to your weaknesses, your failures, your need for improvement, and putting these things into perspective. It also means maintaining a healthy perspective on your achievements, your special talents, and your good works.

This kind of perspective, as I have already indicated, can be summarized in one simple word: *humility*. Unavoidably, thanksgiving and humility go hand in hand. You increase your sense of thankfulness and joy as you maintain an attitude of humility.

Humility is quite simply the recognition that the glow of our lives is a form of reflected radiance, like the moon, rather than a source of light in itself, like the sun. This does not mean that we disparage or minimize our gifts (in fact, we celebrate them), but that we receive them with gratitude, use them with responsibility, and remember always to give credit where credit is due.

Humility is usually thought of as an attitude that downplays our gifts and accomplishments, a kind of "Aw, shucks, ma'am; it was nothin'" response to a compliment. But a true sense of humility is much more subtle than that. It includes a realistic recognition of how much we contributed to both our strengths and our weaknesses. Then it means accepting both accolades and criticism with thanksgiving—because we're not too locked up with pride to accept the input of others.

Here's another vital key to taking ourselves with a grain of salt: laughing at ourselves. The very act of finding humor in both our successes and our failures enables us to get past our pride and maintain a humble and thankful attitude. It's hard to take yourself too seriously when you're laughing at yourself—gently, and with love.

My children and wife do a good job of keeping me humorously aware of my many shortcomings. Many have been the times that I stepped down from the stage after doing a painting demonstration for thousands of collectors, only to have my wife point out with a giggle the stroke of blue paint—looking conspicuously like cheap eyeshadow—that appeared below my eyebrow halfway through the demonstration. Or I will be feeling very pious about what a good father and husband I am, only to have one of my daughters catch me sneaking a cookie five minutes after warning them not to have any sweets before dinner.

As a man who is somewhat in the public eye, I am often concerned that those who enjoy my work might assume that my life and family are perfect. I'm the person who lives with myself every day, so I am acutely aware of just how untrue that is. But one thing I've learned, as I continue to work on my many shortcomings, is that keeping a twinkle in my eye, a smile in my heart, and a humble, thankful attitude about my life is far more helpful than wallowing in guilt or frustration—plus a lot more fun.

THE SECRET OF THE DARK CANVAS

If you happen to be sad, discouraged, or in pain, of course, all this about celebrating your life and remaining humble and chuckling at your shortcomings can seem like a cruel joke. Perhaps you don't have a family. Perhaps your childhood seemed to contribute nothing but pain. Perhaps your ailing body seems to have rebelled against you or your spirits are dragging the ground. You may honestly feel you have nothing to be thankful for.

Even if that's true, I still believe the path to joy for you lies along the way of thankfulness. It's when thankfulness comes hard, in fact, that you most need the lens of gratitude for brightening your life.

How can you manage a thank-you when there's nothing to be thankful for? You can actually say thank you for the darkness. You can choose to be grateful not necessarily for your suffering, your illness, or your sad circumstances, but for the positive effect that even these negative things can have on the larger spectrum of your life.

People who come into my studio when I am in the middle of a painting are often surprised and disappointed to find that a work-in-progress is quite dark, even gloomy—not at all the radiant canvas they expected. I've made it that way on purpose. In fact, I usually spend weeks putting down layer after layer of semitransparent, somber-colored glaze until the whole painting resembles a dreary day or an overcast night—not at all the glowing, sunlit scene I have in the back of my mind.

Why do I deliberately make the painting dark? Because I have learned that the dark layers are a necessary backdrop to the luminous colors I will add at the end. Those dark layers are what will give the work its depth; they will make the windows and the streetlights and even the sun seem to glow from within instead of being dabbed on the surface. Because of the darkness, the light I add has more impact.

Knowing this little secret about light and darkness in painting has helped me be thankful for the dark times in my own life. They add depth to my character to make my joy more radiant. Besides, I know from my experience as a painter and a human being that they won't last. I've discovered, in fact, that my biggest disappointments have often turned into my greatest blessings.

I remember vividly a time when we had decided to fulfill a lifelong dream of living in another part of the country. The only problem was that our house in California just wouldn't sell! It was a quaint little place surrounded by a few acres of property, but nobody seemed to want it. We lived for a year with the "For Sale" sign on the lawn and the house spruced up for visits from the realtor. Finally we decided just to go ahead and visit for an extended period in the area where we wanted to live. We rented rooms and moved in, still feeling the presence of that unsold house like an anchor tied around our necks.

Two weeks later, however, our attitude had completely turned around. Although our intended new village was picturesque and the surrounding

countryside idyllic, the people seemed unfriendly and foreign in their way of thinking. Although we had thought we wanted to experience a new climate, we found ourselves intensely homesick for the temperate weather of our part of California. We missed our home. We missed our families. We didn't want to live in the new area at all.

Suddenly we found ourselves intensely grateful for the gift of that unsold house. Quickly we packed up and moved back to find it and the whole region transformed in our eyes. The faults we had previously focused on seemed unimportant, and we were now aware of many new benefits and advantages we had never noticed before.

If you think about it, you can no doubt remember times like that, when problems turned out to be blessings. Perhaps you failed to get a job you really wanted, only to find a year later that the person who got "your" job was overworked and miserable, and the company you wanted to work for was on the verge of bankruptcy. Or perhaps you gritted your teeth through a painful relational breakup, only to meet the love of your life the very next year. Perhaps an illness or a disability gave you a new appreciation for life or a platform to help others.

All this is not to say that you have to *like* the dark circumstances in your life. The pain, the discouragement, the sadness, the fear, the anger are normal emotions, and denying that they exist will not bring you closer to real happiness. At the same time, understanding that even the "bad" things can be useful gifts, that over time they can increase the quality of radiant light in your life, can help you live through them with gratitude and even, eventually, with joy.

In everything give thanks.
—THE BOOK OF FIRST THESSALONIANS

COUNTING BLESSINGS

I love that old scene from *White Christmas* where Bing Crosby sings to Rosemary Clooney about counting his blessings at night "instead of sheep." I love the image of lying in bed while a flock of wonderful memories leaps by to entertain and delight me.

Counting blessings is a time-honored and trustworthy route to developing a thankful heart, and it's one I practice on a regular basis. In fact, it has become a habit I share with my wife. Many are the times throughout the day that Nanette and I comment in passing on how thankful we are for a certain blessing. We will sit in our backyard, enjoying the lovely flowers and the peaceful shade, and one of us will say, "Aren't you thankful we have this backyard?" Or, as I head out the kitchen door for the fifty-yard "commute" to my studio, I'll often say something to the effect of, "Boy, I'm glad I don't have to fight traffic on the way to work." Somehow, verbalizing our appreciation helps us focus on our advantages rather than on the things we lack or wish we had.

And yes, our home, our cars, our books and clothes and furniture are certainly blessings we appreciate. We enjoy every possession we own. But I can honestly say we had this attitude of thankfulness long before we began to achieve any form of material success. As a newlywed couple in our tiny, drab apartment, with both of us working long hours and living a nocturnal lifestyle just so we could be together, we still spent much of our time counting our blessings—the fact that we had each other, the fact that we had a future, the fact that we each were involved in meaningful, interesting work. We had a place to sleep. We had food to eat. We lived in the center of a bustling, fascinating city. We felt truly blessed, and truly thankful.

This fundamental habit of counting blessings has simply continued to be a part of our lives as we have moved toward the kind of life we once dreamed about. We still have each other. We have four children whom we adore. We love our life, and we are profoundly grateful for our present circumstances. But this sense of gratitude does not depend on specific material blessings. It comes from our habit of counting the blessings, our decision to look at life through the lens of gratitude.

This is not to say we don't have problems. We do. We are reaching the stage in life when we need to think about helping our aging parents. We struggle constantly to keep our family life balanced and private. We have our disagreements. We have our challenges and disappointments. But that's not really the point. No life, even the most blessed, is without problems. But the practice of counting our blessings keeps us focused on enjoying what we have to the fullest and not worrying too much about what we don't have. It's a habit we've managed to practice so long that it's almost become second nature.

And here's another practice I've tried to develop—sort of a reverse way of counting blessings. To me, it's a great way to remind myself that even the frustrations in my life often stem from blessings.

Say that I'm sitting here in my chair, trying to get some quality work done on a painting, but frustrated by the fact that I have a business phone call scheduled in ten minutes. I really don't feel like taking the call. I'm very involved in a detailed area of the painting, I'm a little behind schedule, and I'd much prefer to keep on working.

But when I catch myself grousing about the interruption, I try to counter my own complaint by reframing the irritation in the context of blessing. *Remember when there was no reason to have business calls because you had no business to conduct?* I'll tell myself. *Remember when no one bought your art and you barely had enough to eat? The fact that you have a business call is part of being involved in business.*

Reframing a circumstance in this way, I've found, usually enables me to defuse the irritation. I highly recommend it as a way of turning frustrations into sources of joy.

IMPROVING YOUR COUNTING SKILLS

We aren't born knowing how to count our blessings, any more than we are born knowing how to write and do arithmetic. But it's something anyone can learn, and the habit is well worth developing.

Here's a practical suggestion for teaching yourself the habit of counting blessings. Every morning or night, write a short list of five things you can honestly be thankful for. Keep a special notebook or page just for this purpose. Don't worry if some days you have to struggle to come up with five. If necessary, write down the fact that you are still breathing, that you are not currently sleeping on the streets, that your stomach isn't hurting—whatever you can honestly claim. Just write down the five things, say a brief prayer of thanks, and close the book. The next day, think of five more things. It's all right if they're the same ones you thought of before. But try to think of at least one new blessing.

For the first two weeks that you try this exercise, list *only* five blessings per day. If more occur to you, write only the very best ones.

What will probably happen, if you persist in this exercise, is that the blessings will start lining up in your mind, impatient to be included. You'll find yourself irritated to list only five. You'll find yourself noticing more and more blessings in your life.

After the second week, give yourself permission to make a long list. Write down as many blessings as come to your mind. Let your list scrawl over page after page. When you run out of ideas, just look down at your list and smile. You'll be amazed at the concrete evidence of everything you have to be thankful for.

Or here's another blessings project that can bring you a lot of fun. It's a great spirit lifter on down days, and it's also a great project to do with children. Simply hang a big bulletin board in your foyer or family room and fill it with reminders of everything you have to be thankful for. Add pictures of your family and pets. Tack on mementos from trips or cards from people who care about you. If the brilliance of autumn leaves make you joyful, add a few leaves to your board. If you love the funny papers, pin up some cartoons that make you laugh. Cut out pictures from magazines that remind you of things you are glad for in your life. The point is to fill a visual center with reminders of the blessings in your life.

If you prefer, you can set up a small table or bench and fill it with "favorite things"—a jar of sand from your favorite beach, a sweet-scented candle, some framed photographs, a statue of a puppy dog. Once again, concentrate on creating a visual representation of the blessings that bring you joy in your life.

Once you've created your blessings center, make a point of visiting it from time to time. "Read" your bulletin board. Pick up the items on your table and fondle them. Literally count these blessings that you can see and let them lead your mind on to blessings you can't see. Rejoice in the abundant blessings that fill your life.

And once again, say thank you.

Were there no God, we would be in this glorious world
with grateful hearts and no one to thank.
— CHRISTINA ROSSETTI

THE ACT OF THANK YOU

Here's an interesting phenomenon I've noticed again and again in my own life. The act of expressing my thanks to someone else actually makes me feel more grateful. It solidifies the attitude of thankfulness in my life. If you really want to add the glow of thankfulness to your life, therefore, I recommend some practice in actually expressing your thank-yous. Say it out loud. Write it down on paper. Type it into your computer. Paint it, like I do, onto a piece of canvas.

A good place to start the habit is when you wake up in the morning. Give yourself this challenge as you reach groggily for the alarm clock. Even before you've pushed back the covers, let this thought repeat itself in your mind: *I am thankful for the gift of being alive for another day.* If this simple act of gratitude became your first conscious thought each day, imagine how joyful your life could become.

During the day, you can strengthen your habit of thankfulness by saying

thank you to as many people as you can notice—the man who delivers your paper, the waitress who brings your coffee, your spouse, who lets you in the bathroom first. Remember, there's nothing wrong with thanking people for doing their jobs. Everybody appreciates being noticed and appreciated, and the act of doing it will help you notice all the things that people do for you over the course of a day.

Writing impromptu thank-you notes (not just socially obligated ones) is yet another great way to build the habit of thankfulness in your heart. To help you remember, buy a stack of inexpensive notecards, put stamps on them ahead of time, and place them in a special box or basket along with a pen and perhaps your address book. From time to time during the day, if you happen to think with pleasure of something someone has done for you, take five minutes to jot down a note of thanks and drop it in the mail. If you have trouble getting over to the notecards, send an e-mail or pick up the phone. It doesn't have to be more than, "I was thinking today about how much I enjoyed the book you lent me. Thanks so much."

Finally, regardless of your personal religious beliefs, I think you will find joy in speaking your thanks to whomever or whatever you consider to be the source of your blessings. Pour your thanksgivings out in your prayers, or sit quietly and meditate on your blessings. If prayer and meditation are not part of your personal discipline (or even if they are), try this: Go outside, especially on a beautiful day or a starry night, open your arms, and just say "Thank you" right out loud.

☀

SPEAKING GIFT

Here's one more thing you can do to keep your heart and mind focused with gratitude: You can take up the practice of saying grace.

I don't mean you have to act out a scene from a Dickens novel, posing motionless around the dinner table with hands folded and heads humbly bowed as someone drones out a long table blessing while everyone else's stomach growls. I'm simply suggesting that you set aside a regular time to say a simple thank-you for the many gifts that your life brings you on a daily basis.

There's good reason, of course, that in many cultures this practice has come to be associated with mealtimes. Meals can provide a regular, dependable cue for thanks. Our family has long been in the habit of pausing before we eat, holding hands, and saying a prayer of gratitude for the gifts of food and family. Frequently, my children will add a special mention of thanks all their own. In fact, my three-year-old often gets a little too enthusiastic in her prayers and has to be reminded that it's time to eat! Even so, the ritual of saying grace has come to have great meaning for us as a routine reminder of how much we have to be thankful for.

But you can practice saying grace at other times, too, by choosing a regular event in your life as a cue for saying regular thank-yous. Our family often celebrates our safe arrival home from a journey with a little statement of thanks. And we try to end each day with a brief prayer of thanksgiving before turning off the bedroom lights.

If you are in the habit of enjoying a cup of morning tea, try saying thanks while the tea is steeping. If you exercise after work every day, consider whispering a thank-you whenever you leave the gym. (Some days, you may find yourself saying thank you that you're through with your workout!) Although this practice may seem artificial or strange to you at first, I believe you'll find that those few seconds of conscious, verbalized thankfulness truly make a difference in your life.

In my experience, at least, saying grace has been a tremendously helpful way to keep myself looking through the rosy lens of gratitude. It's only recently, though, that I've begun to wonder why this habit of formally verbalizing a thank-you is actually called "saying grace."

As I've thought about it, I've come to realize what a wealth of meaning lies in those two little words — *saying grace* — a meaning that can transform anyone's life, regardless of whether they feel inclined to say prayers at mealtimes.

Grace, you see, is another word for an unearned gift, and a large part of every person's life falls into that category. It is only by grace that we are here on this planet. It is only by grace that we are who we are. And although we can attribute much of our good or bad fortune to our actions, so much of what we enjoy on a daily basis is also a gift of grace, something for which we can take only limited credit.

Saying grace is simply the act of admitting that fact out loud. Quite literally, when we say grace, we are "speaking gift." Whether we are saying a formal blessing before a meal or a quiet thank-you whispered into a teacup, we are owning up to the fact that our histories, our current circumstances, the possibilities that lie before us are all part of the wonderful gift that is our life. For a gift like that, the only proper response is "Thank you."

When I look at my life through the lens of gratitude,
all my experiences take on a rosy glow.

LIGHTPOSTS
FOR LIVING

Ten

A RADIANT SUNRISE

LIVING IN A ROMANTIC LIGHT

Life's a banquet, and most poor suckers are starving to death.
—AUNTIE MAME (PATRICK DENNIS)

"Romance isn't everything."

You've probably been told that at one time or another in your life. You may have said it yourself, or something like it—most likely to protect yourself or someone else from disappointment or thwarted hopes. Despite the valiant efforts of the card companies, we live in a profoundly unromantic age. There seems to be a widespread assumption that seeking romance is really courting disaster.

I beg to differ—vehemently. I resist the cynical or sad assumption that romance is nothing but sentimental claptrap or an invitation to a broken heart. I believe, in fact, that keeping a spark of romance in your heart is one of the more important keys to living a joyful life.

But don't misunderstand me. Most especially, don't start feeling left out if you happen to be "between relationships," if no one remembered you on Valentine's Day, or if you've been told you don't have a romantic nature.

We *all* have a romantic nature of one kind or another buried somewhere in our hearts. Deep inside, I think most of us yearn for a life that is full of extraordinary experiences and graced with beauty and charm. That's what a romantic life is really all about. And all it takes to live this life is a little passion, a little imagination, and a willingness to stretch our minds beyond the romantic stereotypes of ruffles and flourishes. Then we can all embrace the larger-than-life joy that comes from even a touch of romance.

The way I see it, we do romance a disservice by limiting its meaning to the "chemistry" between lovers, the traditional trappings of courtship (hearts and flowers), and a certain style of old-fashioned living (afternoon tea and cabbage roses). As much as I personally appreciate romantic friendship (my wife can testify that I'm an incurable romantic), as much as I love sentimental things like hearts and flowers (more, perhaps, than she does), I hate to see this grand old word reduced to such a meager shadow of its former self.

Romance encompasses so much more than the spark of love between sweethearts and the trappings of a bygone age. In a much more basic sense, it is the quality that adds a feeling of a radiant sunrise to every aspect of living. It properly refers to an attitude that gives life its energy and zest, its wide-eyed enthusiasm.

To be romantic, in other words, is quite simply to allow yourself to fall in love with life—all of life—and experience it fully, openly, passionately, and purposefully.

That kind of romance might not be everything, but I believe it's an essential part of a joyful life.

THREE FACES OF ROMANCE

What does it mean, specifically, to live a romantic life in this bigger, more encompassing sense?

First of all, I believe, a romantic life includes an element of exploration and adventure. A romantic is a person who appreciates and seeks after rich and varied experiences. He or she is likely to be intensely curious, energetically interested in what the world has to offer. Romantics love the unusual and the odd and the undiscovered—whether in the little antique shop down the road, the unexplored pathway behind the subdivision, or the hidden depths of someone they love. They believe there is always something new to be learned, always another memory to be made, always the enticing possibility of some kind of adventure to be enjoyed.

Travel appeals to this aspect of the romantic soul. Some people thrive on hiking the trails, riding the rails, exploring the backroads. Others prefer arm-

chair travel, reading books and watching films about far-away places. Both means of exploring can add romantic spice to our usual worlds of twice-a-day commutes and journeys to the supermarket.

Discovering new possibilities close to home is another kind of adventure that can make a life romantic. Our family once made a list of little cafés and greasy spoon restaurants that had piqued our curiosity in the town where we lived. Over a period of months, we visited every one—checking it off our list as we experienced its peculiar chrome-and-vinyl atmosphere and the down-at-the-heel charm of its wait staff and regular clientele. That time of discovery, which never took us more than twenty miles from home, inspired our whole family with a sense of adventurous fun. And adventurous fun is a big part of the truly romantic life.

The pleasures of the senses, too, contribute to a romantic life. And don't shy away from the term *sensual* as though it were somehow illicit or degrading. Sensual pleasure is quite simply the capacity to find delight through the senses—and a romantic life is inescapably "sensual."

The beautiful clothing and furnishings and decorations we have come to think of as "romantic" (a dainty, jeweled stickpin, a gauzy gown, a colorful antique throw rug) certainly fit this description. So can a pot of herbs in a windowsill, a luscious-smelling strawberry, a jazz CD on the stereo, a gentle breeze wafting through a window. And so, of course, can the presence and the touch of one's beloved.

To be romantic is to allow yourself to remain sensually open to the beauties of the world around you—intensely alive to the big and little enjoyments that life has to offer to eye, ear, nose, tongue, and skin. And there is an accompanying sense of being *imaginatively* open as well, enlisting the mind and the heart in the active enjoyment of every moment.

There is also a higher calling in a romantic life, a heartfelt dedication to the belief that life has meaning beyond the banal. A true romantic is a person who places high value on a good deed, a lovely gesture, a noble sentiment, or a heroic aspiration. He or she is one whose heart beats faster at the idea of attempting something extraordinary.

This, in fact, is perhaps the oldest meaning of the word *romantic*. It is the stuff of legends, of noble deeds and timeless quests. It is an old-fashioned value scorned by cynical society—and sorely needed, I believe, in a joy-starved world. We *need* the sense that our reach can exceed our grasp. We *need* something to believe in, something to inspire us to be better than we are.

This aspect of the romantic life brings to mind Don Quixote, tilting crazily at windmills but at least attempting something grand and wonderful. It recalls Romantic painters and poets of the nineteenth century celebrating life on huge canvases and in reams of heroic verse. It echoes the passion of the French underground during World War II or the courage of civil rights freedom marchers.

But the noble calling of romance exists on a small scale as well as a large one. This close-in dimension may actually have more meaning to those of us who aspire to a romantic life. Romance is found not only in the sacrifice of one's freedom for the sake of a principle, but also in the sacrifice of an afternoon for the sake of a relationship. It is the quest for a thoughtful gift as well as the search for the Holy Grail. It is the supremely sacrificial gesture of surrendering not only one's heart, but also one's energy and time. Doing a small, loving thing with beautiful panache can be every bit as romantic as committing a heroic deed with nobility and honor.

All's cold and grey without it. They that have had it have slipped in and out of heaven.
—J. M. Barrie

No Excuses

Your life is not likely to be the stuff of epics. But the sparkle and spice of adventurous discovery, sensual pleasure, and even noble endeavor can easily be woven into the fabric of your days.

How? Begin by affirming the fact that you are entitled to a romantic life. Resist the temptation to protest that "real life is just not that way." Give up the excuses that you are too tired, that you don't have time, or that your spouse just isn't interested in romance. It's enough that *you're* interested.

You are infinitely deserving of the quality of romance in your life. You qualify for adventure and discovery. You are entitled to pleasure and delight in whatever form will make you happy without compromising your integrity. You are up to the challenge of a noble gesture or at least a good deed. It is perfectly appropriate for you to live with zest and enthusiasm and to experience life beyond the mundane—and you have the ability to make it happen.

So begin your quest for romantic living by actively and unashamedly romancing your life! Whatever romantic elements speak to your wistful yearnings or make your heart beat faster—from moonlit walks on the beach to wispy Victorian shawls, from epic poetry in old leatherbound volumes to mountain climbing on weekends—these are the elements to seek out and make a part of you.

If your romantic partner isn't interested in such things, seek them out for yourself. (He or she will still benefit from the new spark of romance in your eyes.) If you feel awkward seeking adventure alone, find a friend who shares your interest. If you don't have anyone to guide you up that mountain, sign up for a climbing expedition.

Don't let the excuse of no energy get in your way, either. Romancing your life is a key to getting *more* energy. A small investment of time and effort yields huge returns of zest and enthusiasm. The very act of pursuing romance will give you more energy for making your life even more romantic.

Besides, I have learned that there are many alternate paths to a romantic existence. You really may not have the physical stamina to climb Mt. Shasta, for instance. But you can curl up in a comfortable armchair and lose yourself in a book about the conquest of Everest. Even better, you can take your book on an expedition to find a fascinating, out-of-the-way coffee shop where you can read over cappuccino and watch the people come and go. Or you could make a goal to get in shape so that you can learn real mountain climbing. With very few exceptions, if you can dream it, you can find a way to do it.

Beware especially of the excuse that "I tried it before and was disappointed." This excuse, of course, is often used by those who have had a relationship that didn't work out. But it has also been trotted out to avoid traveling because the car once broke down five hundred miles from home or to justify not taking a break from work because an afternoon to bake bread ended up producing a panful of charcoal briquettes. Such disappointments are simply part of life; it's not fair to blame them on romance. And while it is true that pursuing a romantic life may leave you more vulnerable to feeling the disappointment, it is also true that failed adventures can make the most interesting memories.

Life is meant to be *lived*—that's the essence of the romantic's creed. And living by definition will include its share of pain. That's no excuse for passing up the joy of romance. It staggers me to see the number of people who seem to choose lives that are empty and without zest. What a waste of precious days and minutes!

I urge you, therefore, to resist the temptation always to play it safe. Start romancing your life, and I think you'll find that more romance will follow.

FEATHER YOUR ROMANTIC NEST

Perhaps the easiest and most basic way to make your life more romantic is to surround yourself with objects and ideas that fuel the romantic fire within you. Your home is the place, especially, to caress your senses with beauty and fill your mind with inspiration.

Does your heart respond to antique lace and filigreed silver? Haunt thrift stores for beautiful old pieces to decorate your bedroom or even your bath.

Do you love Chinese figurines or Native American pottery? Visit import stores and gift shops for inexpensive reproductions or save up for authentic pieces. You might even want to combine your vacations with treasure hunts, as I often do, and seek out the kinds of items that will heighten the romantic atmosphere in your home.

Does your spirit lift when you encounter tales of derring-do? Stack up a collection of adventure novels beside your old leather armchair, switch on a lamp with an amber shade, and lose yourself for a couple of hours. Or, if you prefer, gather your family for an evening of old Westerns or science fiction classics on the VCR.

Poetry, I have found, is one of the least utilized forms of fuel for the romantic heart. I myself am partial to Emerson and Wordsworth, but you may prefer Shakespeare sonnets or even Shel Silverstein. Whatever your taste, the products of a poetic imagination can add to the sense of romance in your life. Why not keep a book by your bedside? Better yet, take a quilt into the backyard this Saturday, stretch out beneath a tree, and sip lemonade while you read the verses aloud to yourself or to someone you love.

Music, too, seems to have special romantic power. Keep a supply of audiotapes or CDs close at hand, perhaps in a decorative basket. Stock up on Lizst and Debussy or Johnny Mathis or Garth Brooks—whatever leaves *you* feeling more excited about the experience of living. Perhaps you could save up for a piano or a guitar—or even a harp—and take lessons in making beautiful music. And you might want to invest in other kinds of romantic sounds as well. You can fill your home with romantic sounds by hanging a tinkling wind chime or plugging in a miniature fountain from a garden shop.

Romance is a state of mind.
If you have the right mindset, you can make cleaning the bathroom romantic;
if you have the wrong mindset, you can turn a moonlit stroll on the beach into a fight.
—GREGORY J. P. GODEK

Have you ever thought of nurturing your spiritual life as a romantic exercise? If you define romance as adventure and discovery and even the search for the good, a spiritual quest certainly qualifies as a romantic one. While you are in the process of feathering your romantic nest, why not set aside a special corner as a kind of household altar, a place you seek out for spiritual renewal.

Nanette's tea chair serves this purpose; this is where she sits and sips tea and reads her Bible. A bedside table serves the same purpose for a friend who keeps it stocked with a candle and a small stack of inspirational books. Another friend has even set aside a room in her house as a spiritual retreat, filling it with sights, sounds, and objects that help her journey within—a kneeling bench, a small fountain, and a small tape player that plays Gregorian chant.

Feathering your romantic nest means more than just decorating, however. It also means investing your daily activities with a sense of ritual and drama—setting yourself up to *experience* them instead of just *doing* them.

At mealtime, for instance, at least some of the time, set the table carefully and completely—with beautiful linens, your best dishes, a centerpiece, and perhaps even candles. Plan to make the dinner an event rather than a mundane ritual. And do this for yourself and your family, not just for guests.

At bedtime, too, you can mark the transition into sleep in a romantic or even dramatic way. Slip into the bedroom ahead of time to turn down the sheets. On chilly nights, turn on an electric blanket an hour or two before bedtime and enjoy the luxurious warmth as you snuggle in later. During the summer, place a bouquet on the bedstand and enjoy the delicate fragrance all night long. If you like, you could even park a steaming mug of vanilla-flavored warm milk on the nightstand—a lovely romantic gift for yourself or for the one you love.

With a little imagination, you can learn to celebrate all the hours of your home life (or even your office life) romantically. Instead of wolfing down a candy bar to boost your energy in the late afternoon, why not enjoy a traditional English teatime complete with china cups and saucers, little sugar cubes, and dainty, crustless sandwiches? Or ease the hectic transition of the come-home-and-get-ready-for-dinner time with a family "happy hour" that features quiet music, savory snacks, and perhaps an outdoor game with the kids while your spouse puts the finishing touches on the evening meal.

Obviously, the specific ways that you feather your romantic nest will vary according to who you are. But don't feel obliged to adhere to the typical images of romance—unless hearts and flowers truly fire the romantic spark in your soul.

A kitchen full of exotic spices, wonderful utensils, and unusual cookbooks can be profoundly romantic, encouraging you to explore new worlds of culinary delight. A romantic child's room can be adorned with storybook posters and painted with clouds and stars—stoking the imaginations of children and parents alike. Even your morning shower can be a celebration. I for one enjoy it when my wife purchases one of those luxurious scented shampoos. Nothing wakes up the spirit like apricot bubbles in your hair first thing in the morning!

Do you see the point? Your home will be a romantic hideaway—every detail of it—when you think through the romantic moments you can live there and when you set the stage of your home environment for romance.

PLANNING YOUR ROMANCE

It's a myth that the most romantic experiences are spontaneous ones.

Often, in fact, the most wonderful, romantic events are those that are planned most carefully.

What's the difference between a perfect romantic evening and just another meal? The difference lies in the fact that you looked forward all day to the occasion. The difference lies in the fact that you dressed carefully and splashed yourself with scent. The difference lies in the fact that you reserved a table next to the fountain and made sure the strolling violinist would be on duty when you arrived. The difference lies in the fact that you saved for weeks to be able to afford the meal.

Planning stimulates romance by getting the details right—the spray of orchids or the single, fragrant rose, the perfect gift of an out-of-print book or a bottle of favorite perfume, the horse-drawn carriage that you made sure would be waiting outside. Planning heads off romance-chilling distractions and disappointments—losing your keys, not getting a seat, not knowing what to talk about. It also frees you to enjoy the romantic outing because the practical details (such as baby-sitting) have been taken care of.

And planning also allows for what I consider the most romantic experience of all—anticipation. To me, a romantic adventure is most delicious when

I can daydream about it ahead of time, trying the possibilities on in my mind, thinking of what we will do and what we might say. By the time the moment arrives to begin, my enthusiasm has been whetted by anticipation, and my enjoyment of the event is intensified.

This magic of anticipation especially holds true for me when it comes to travel. Half the fun—for me, at least—lies in planning the trip. I love to pore over maps and travel books, dreaming of places we might visit. I love to daydream about what the trip will be like and what we might discover. If possible, I like to pick up a smattering of the language or a bit of local culture. Even packing is fun for me; I love the challenge of packing just the right clothes and books and painting tools.

But this kind of careful planning is not the same thing as rigid regimentation. The purpose of planning is to clear up details ahead of time and give you time to anticipate the event, not to try to control what will happen. Once embarked upon a romantic experience, in fact, I often like to let life lead, changing my plans as I need to, responding to the experience of the moment.

Thus a romantic restaurant dinner with Nanette might turn into an evening at a jazz club or a quiet walk through our hometown, peeking in all the shop windows. A family vacation to a mountain town might turn into a side trip to a pioneer village or an expedition through a local cave.

Quite often, in fact, our family will start out to go one place and end up somewhere else entirely. That doesn't mean we didn't plan carefully; it simply means we gave ourselves permission to change our minds and follow our hearts. And this, to us at least, is a very romantic proposition.

Hitting just the right balance between careful planning and footloose spontaneity will depend to a great extent on personality and taste. Some people love surprises and thrive on spontaneity. (I do.) Other people prefer to have a little advance notice. (Nanette does.) Some people like to spell out every detail. Other people prefer to sketch out the overall plan and let the details take care of themselves. For maximum romantic mileage, though, I think it's good to remember that even surprises can be improved with a little planning, and that the most carefully planned events could use a little spontaneity.

And remember, once again, that these romantic rules apply to things you do for yourself as well as things you do with someone special. A dinner or vacation for one can be just as carefully planned, as eagerly anticipated, and as spontaneously changed as a dinner or vacation for two or more.

Even if you are used to being part of a couple, in fact, you might be surprised at the delicious luxury of planning an entire day just for yourself. Try it the next time your husband or wife is out of town. Hire a sitter, pull out your planner, and schedule yourself for a morning, noon, and night of doing entirely what pleases you.

Do you love the idea of a lazy morning reading books and munching fruit? Pencil it in. Have you been meaning to go to that new show at the art museum? Schedule a visit (but don't be afraid to change your mind and go to the zoo instead!). Ride your bike to a little deli for lunch and then follow your nose to a few of the great little shops nearby. Sit on a park bench and watch people; you can actually schedule time to do just that. Make a reservation for one at a restaurant you've always wanted to try, or serve yourself a single portion of your favorite dinner on your best china. Then take yourself to a movie or play, come home to a warm bubble bath, and tuck yourself into bed.

Sound wonderful? Why not try it?

Simply make a plan, let yourself look forward to a wonderful time, give yourself permission to follow an alternate path . . . and enjoy a rich, rewarding, romantic experience just for you.

> *A psychiatrist friend of ours makes this statement: One test of emotional health*
> *is the ability to say "Yes," "No," and "Whoopee."*
> —CHARLIE SHEDD AND MARTHA SHEDD

SOMETIMES SPLURGE

It really doesn't take much to make your life more romantic. Small gestures, small events, small experiences, often mean the most. They don't have to be expensive. Often the most lovely things cost very little or nothing at all.

A picnic in the park, for instance, can be soul-stirringly romantic. So can a Saturday at the roller rink. A stolen moment between appointments can help keep a romantic relationship humming. Even a quiet evening at home with a bowl of popcorn and an old movie can be an intensely romantic experience.

But if you want the joy of romance to bloom fully, sometimes you have to pull out the stops and do something extravagant; you need to be willing to splurge a little. I don't just mean spending money, although a dozen roses or a surprise ski weekend can be both expensive and extravagantly romantic. The most important romantic extravagance, however, is an extravagance of time and of feeling. You have to be willing to risk yourself, to give yourself fully. You need to enlist your imagination to add the extra touches that turn a nice time into a romantic extravaganza. Every once in a while, to maintain the spark of romance in a life or a relationship, a grand gesture is called for — like buying a car just to go on a date!

That's one of our family legends, the account of Nanette's and my first date after a long separation. I was thrilled to be back in touch with my high school sweetheart, and I couldn't wait to see her again. The only problem was that I lived five hundred miles away, with no transportation except a battered motorcycle. And I had just two days to get to Nanette's, show her the time of her life, and get back to work on Monday morning.

My most logical course of action was clear to me. First, I had to drain my savings and buy a car with a good tape deck to play our favorite romantic music. (A rental car wouldn't do; as a young artist just starting his career, I needed to show financial stability!) Second, I had to drive the five hundred miles to pick up Nanette, drive her another two hundred miles for dinner and dancing at Lake Tahoe, then take her home and get myself back to Los Angeles in time for work. I proceeded to do all of the above, and I arrived at the movie studio where I worked as a background artist with a few hours to spare, having gone more than forty hours without sleep.

That date, as far as I can tell, cost me more than seven thousand dollars! And it was just the beginning of many more marathon dates, when Nanette and I would drive long distances, talk through the nights, and then hurry to return to our weekday lives. Before long, those long talks began to center upon plans for a life together.

I am certainly not recommending that you spend your life savings for a romantic gesture. That was truly a once-in-a-lifetime event! And yet, in a sense, that particular grand gesture determined the course of our lives together.

Sometimes, in other words, you just have to splurge — with your money, your imagination, your heart, or all three.

Sometimes, instead of sending a card, you need to hire an airplane to do some sky writing. Sometimes, instead of sending a balloon bouquet, you need to fill a whole room with balloons. Sometimes, instead of lunch under the arches, you need to pack a seven-course meal in a basket and enjoy it under the elms. Sometimes, instead of a trip to the next town, you need to take a trip on the Orient Express.

There's something about the willingness to go all out, at least occasionally, that reminds us how big and abundant life can be. Besides, it's the big gestures, most of the time, that give us the best stories to tell our grandchildren.

And yes, there is a certain danger in extravagance. You may risk running out of money or time. You risk being misunderstood or even laughed at.

But usually, the danger is minimal. Even if it isn't—that's exactly the point. That element of risk is what makes the gesture extravagant—and irresistibly romantic.

PAY ATTENTION

This, I believe, is the most important key to a more romantic life: You have to be willing to pay attention.

In a romantic relationship, the gestures and gifts that matter most are the ones that show that one person is really receptive to the other person's wants and needs. When I send Nanette a bouquet of flowers, she's happy. But when I remember to arrive home ten minutes early and take the kids for a walk, freeing her to collect her thoughts before dinner, then Nanette is *really* happy. The romance of the latter gesture lies in my realizing that what my wife needs most these days is help with her busy and demanding schedule as the mother of four small children. What makes it *really* romantic is the fact that I do it without being asked. (And no, I don't always remember, but I am learning!)

This element of paying attention is exactly what lends a romantic quality to cooking her favorite meal or bringing home tickets to a concert by his favorite musician. Romance is sending yellow roses instead of pink ones because you remember that's what she buys for herself. It's picking up an antique lamp in a curio shop because, in an idle moment, he once mentioned that he might like to start a collection.

Paying attention is also what lends a romantic quality to your relationship with yourself. You romance your own life by paying attention to what kinds of experiences bring you energy and inspiration. Your life takes on a romantic glow when you give yourself permission to please yourself.

The most meaningful aspect of any such gesture is that it shows *attentive-ness*. Attentiveness to another person means tuning down the clamor of your own needs enough to respond to his or her needs and desires. It displays a willingness to speak, as it were, in another person's language, to do the things the other person likes, the things that mean the most to her or him. Being attentive to yourself, on the other hand, means tuning down the clamor of demands and expectations that assault you daily so that you can respond to your own needs. It means being willing to spend some time and money to make your own life feel special and out of the ordinary. Paying loving attention to your own needs as well as the needs of others is a supremely romantic gesture.

Most important of all, even more important than being attentive, is simply to be *present* in the moment, not letting yourself be distracted by thoughts of what happened earlier in the day or what you've got planned next week. This is not always easy, but it's a skill worth developing. After all, the moment is the only place where we can actually live — where we can experience life at its fullest and most romantic.

In the long run, it's not just hearts and flowers, but the willingness and ability to *open* your heart and to *smell* the flowers that makes your life truly romantic.

And that's a life, I promise you, that you wouldn't want to miss.

Romance makes a radiant sunrise out of every moment.

LIGHTPOSTS
FOR LIVING

ELEVEN

LIGHT A FRESH CANDLE

LIVING IN THE LIGHT OF CREATIVITY

Thou takest the pen — and the lines dance.
Thou takest the flute — and the notes shimmer.
Thou takest the brush — and the colors sing. . . .
How, then, can I hold back anything from Thee.
— DAG HAMMARSKJÖLD

Creativity, you might say, is my business.

As a professional artist, I make my living from dreaming up worlds that never really existed and bringing them to life on canvas. Creativity is a tool of my trade, just as surely as my brushes and pigments are. In a sense, it is also my stock-in-trade, because I make a living by selling the fruits of my creativity.

But would you be surprised if I told you that creativity is *your* business, too?

Unless you happen to make your living the way I do, that statement might take you aback. You might even feel compelled to begin cataloging your artistic failings: "But I can't draw." "I can't sing." "I'm just not the creative type." Or you might immediately think of your current life and wonder how creativity could have anything to do with the way you sell fabric or punch rivets or type reports or deliver newspapers.

Creativity has everything to do with the way you live, because creativity is the essence of your heritage as a human being. It's impossible for you *not* to be creative, at least when it comes to your potential. You were born to take the raw materials of your life and continually mold them into something new, something unique, something that has never existed in that particular configuration since the dawn of history.

Your creation doesn't have to be a painting—although, obviously, I believe painting is an appropriate creative endeavor. It doesn't have to be a poem or a sonata or a marble statue or any other kind of traditional artistic work. Creativity can also produce a salmon mousse, a jet propulsion system, a crossword puzzle, or a Japanese garden. It can unsnarl a business snafu or forge a workable truce between warring nations. It can come up with the perfect way to encourage a sullen teenager or to brighten a lackluster apartment with a splash of colored quilt.

Creativity can even shape or reshape an entire life—as I learned from a dear friend, a former teacher of mine.

This man was one of those legendary high school English teachers—eccentric, passionate about his subject, both adored and feared by his students. He made a lasting impression on generations of high school kids, including my brother and me. But when he retired, this teacher was faced with the dilemma of what to do with the rest of his life. He had no family. He wasn't really the type to play golf or travel continuously. But he did love books. So my friend made what I consider to be a truly creative decision: He took up the hobby of bookbinding and book repair. Once he learned the secrets of replacing torn leather and restoring broken spines, he began taking in books from anyone who would bring them, making them once more fit for active use. He often spoke of this service as the "Old Friends Repair Club." Not surprisingly, his skills were soon in demand at the local public library.

Then this retired teacher had another creative idea. He approached the local hospice association with the idea of using his book-repair skills for fundraising purposes. Now he manages a little book area in the hospice thrift store. He and a small band of volunteers restore thousands of books every year and then resell them, with all profits going to the hospice. The last time I spoke with him, my friend proudly confided that in the last year alone, his service had raised more than $30,000 for the hospice!

I consider that a pretty good return for a couple of creative decisions. Not only have countless "old friends" received a new lease on life, but a worthy organization has also been able to expand its programs, and a retired teacher has found new joy and purpose in his later years—all because of a little creativity.

I have come to believe that creativity isn't optional for any human being. It is a daily part of our lives, no matter our age, our background, or our abilities. It's the gift that enables us to solve our problems, to move from point A to points B or C or Z, to explore the full depth and potential of the human experience.

Every time you attempt to solve a problem, you're being creative. Every time you try a new path, invent a new approach, craft a new object, you are rearranging the raw materials of your life into something new—and that's the essence of creativity. You are using your mind, your imagination, your hands, and your spiritual connection to make something that has never existed before in that particular combination. Creativity is what separates us from other species—an ongoing way of emulating the Creator himself, who when he finished his task looked about and said, "It is good."

With every creative act, you light a fresh candle for a darkened world—and that in itself is a powerful source of joy for your life.

FILL YOUR MIND AND HEART

How do you enhance the creative power in your life? This subject has been a particular passion of mine over the years, and I'd like to share a few simple techniques that have helped me immensely.

I believe the most important thing to remember is that nothing comes from nothing. Creative output must begin with creative input. The starting point for all creative acts, in other words, is to live life and pay attention!

Children's book author Katherine Paterson once said that she doesn't believe in "writer's block." In her experience, the thing that freezes a writer's soul and leaves her staring in panic at a blank computer screen is writer's *starvation*. I think that applies to any other kind of creative endeavor as well. If you are having trouble coming up with a fresh idea or a new approach to a problem—or even if you're just trying to get a little more creative "juice" into your hobbies, your work, and your life—the first thing to do is to fill your mind and heart with sights, sounds, ideas, images, experiences.

At the simplest level, head outdoors and really look at the world around you. Notice the ants on the sidewalk, the hawks in the treetops, the sprinklers on the lawn. Observe the people who pass. Talk to your neighbor on the corner or the old man who sits on the park bench. Read billboards. Notice the feel of your own heart pumping and your feet moving in your sneakers. None of these observations and experiences will be wasted. They are the raw materials of your creative life.

The greatest of the practiced arts is to live life deeply, fully.
— KAREN BURTON MAINS

In addition to observing, you can increase your creative store by reading everything you can get your hands on, everything from vintage comics to great world masterpieces. Read children's books. Read mystery novels and travelogues. Pore through dusty tomes from used bookstores and shining new titles from the corner bookstand. Or do what I love to do: Spend a spare hour poring through dusty old magazines. (I buy these at antique stores and used bookstores and really enjoy the glimpse they give of life in an earlier era.)

One practice I find especially stimulating and helpful as a creative tool is to read books and articles by people whose opinions and beliefs are different from mine. I enjoy reading divergent points of view on a given hotly debated issue. As a Christian, I find my own beliefs are clarified in my mind by reading books by people of different faiths or those with no particular spiritual foundation. I find that this simple determination to open myself to the input of people with differing viewpoints not only sharpens me intellectually, but also helps open me up creatively by keeping me out of a mental rut.

Sitting down to read, of course, is not the only way to experience the creative input of others. You can also "listen" to literature—anything from a set of essays to a Dickens novel—on tape. (I know many people who appreciate this kind of input when they drive. My own prime time for listening is when I'm doing repetitive work at my easel.) Music, too, can be a rich source of creative inspiration, whether you listen to it on the stereo, the radio, or in live concert. You can fill your mind with a rich mélange of ideas and images by watching films or attending theater performances. Museums, too, are wonderful creativity resources—especially the odd little museums you often find off the beaten track. How can one visit the guillotine museum in Paris, the dog collar museum in England, or even the Superman museum in Metropolis, Illinois, and not find creative material to feed the imagination?

I personally find that visual input is vital to my own creativity. I glean ideas and inspiration from anything that meets my eye, so I take pains to surround myself with interesting visual experiences. I have an entire work library full of art books —volumes of pictures and words that bring me instant inspiration as I browse through them. The pictures that grace my studio walls — ranging from paintings by people I know and admire to a small collection of antique Russian icons to a grouping of my own early work—

are there for the purposes of creative and spiritual inspiration. When I travel, I try not to miss an opportunity to visit galleries and art museums, studying the work of those who have gone before me. And I keep my own plein air studies (quick paintings done from nature) and my works in progress out in full view when I work—I'll often get an idea just from seeing a piece on the mantel or propped against the wall.

One of my most valuable visual resources is my idea board, where I tack up random thoughts, sketches, magazine pictures anything that intrigues me or suggests creative possibilities. I keep this idea board in plain sight while I work, and I am constantly in the process of arranging it and rearranging it—adding things, taking away things, bringing some items to the front, moving others together in groups.

This very process of handling objects is yet another thing that seems to get my creative juices flowing. I've tried over the years to fill my home and studio with small statues, clay jars, antique knickknacks, and other objects I can easily pick up and handle while I walk around and think. I find that I think most creatively with this hands-on approach. I run my hands over an object, handle its surfaces, and somehow new ideas and associations begin popping up.

One of the most fruitful "creative" sources in my life is people. I love to spend time with those who are in the process of putting new things together. I find my mind and creativity stimulated by conversations with other artists, interactions with writers, conferences with creative businesspeople. When I have time, I love to visit crafts fairs and discover emerging artisans, talk to the chefs at restaurants I visit, and simply enjoy conversations with my friends. Such conversations often provide both energy and ideas to fuel my creative work.

You may well find, of course, that your best sources of creative input differ from mine. Whereas I tend to respond to what I see and touch, you may respond more to what you hear. Perhaps music is the key to bringing out your creative gift. Or perhaps you will derive your most inventive ideas from simply sitting in a coffee shop and listening to people talk or from finding a mentor in your chosen creative endeavor.

"The world is so full of a number of things," wrote Robert Louis Stevenson, "I'm sure we should all be as happy as kings." That's good advice for the creative process as well. If you want to live more creatively and more joyfully, you'll surround yourself with "a number of things." You'll look at them, touch them, smell them, listen to them, think about them. When your heart and mind are full, you'll be well on the way toward awakening the joy of creativity.

DON'T LET IT GET AWAY

You never know when an idea will strike. Creative inspirations are just as likely to hit while you're standing in the shower or washing the dishes as when you are sitting at a desk or easel. I've found that these moments of inspiration are powerful but fleeting. Often, if I wait to get them down in some form, they'll be gone. So I learned long ago to grab a towel, dry my

hands, and then, as quickly as possible, to capture the idea on paper. Once I've made a note or laid down a quick thumbnail sketch, I go right back to what I was doing, relieved that the idea is saved and waiting for my use.

This concept of capturing ideas when they occur is so important to me that I had a notebook custom made for this purpose. It's a blank book made of quality sketch paper and tucked into a leather cover with a holder for a pen. But you don't have to have a notebook specially made; any device that is small enough to carry around and sturdy enough to use on a regular basis will do. I know people who record all their brainstorms in the notes section of their daily organizers. Some like to keep index cards in their pockets. A few carry handheld computers or even little tape recorders to capture notes on the fly. The medium doesn't really matter. What *does* matter is having a convenient place to record all your ideas and training yourself to carry it with you everywhere.

In addition to carrying a notebook, almost every creative person I know recommends keeping a journal of some sort—a place where you regularly reflect on the events of your life. I have been a journaler off and on since childhood, and I find that the very act of filling the pages often stirs up ideas that will eventually emerge in a painting.

When most people think of journals, of course, they think of feelings poured out in words, but there's more than one way to process experience creatively. Scrapbooks, photograph albums, even file folders of clippings can serve a similar purpose. Try pressing leaves and flowers collected on your hikes and pressing them into an album. Or fill the margins of a travel guide with your personal notes about your travels.

My sketchpads are in essence visual journals, collected studies of things I have observed—a woman waiting for a bus, a tree with an interesting knothole, the neighbor's dog. You don't have to be an artist to benefit from the habit of recording what you see in this way. The sketches don't have to be technically accomplished, any more than a written journal entry has to be of literary quality. Their primary value is in pushing your brain to react to the world in a different way; you see something differently when you try to sketch it, and this in itself helps you be more creative.

Or here's another journal idea you may not have thought of: other people! I've often thought that my relationship with my wife is almost like a journal of my life. I don't really feel I've experienced something until I've shared it with Nanette in some way, and the very act of talking with her about what is going on in our lives seems to help me sort out my thoughts and observations for later creative use.

I think that many people, especially those who are more extroverted, pick up creative energy from this kind of verbal interaction. If that's true for you, I urge you to make good use of it. Consider yourself blessed if you have a friend, colleague, or loved one you trust enough to be a living journal in your life.

THE HARD WORK OF CREATIVITY

Here's a hard truth about creativity, one you probably already know: It's not all brainstorms and flashes of insight. Some of it is just plain old work—often joyful, sometimes thrilling, frequently dull, occasionally excruciating. For any creative endeavor, you have to be willing to put in some effort developing an idea or laying the groundwork for ideas to come.

A college professor I know who does a lot of writing refers to the requisite prep work of creativity as rear-in-chair time. It's the time when she actually sits at her desk putting together outlines, looking through sources, roughing out chapters, correcting the ones she's written. For me, this rear-in-chair time is more likely to be sitting-at-easel time, spent developing the way a painting is going to work. It's also research time, when I check out the architecture of a certain building, the make of a vintage car, the forms of flowers and foliage. It is the work I do to make my paintings visually accurate and technically sound. And it absolutely has to be done if something new is to be created. Sometimes it has to be done before an idea can even emerge.

It is handed to you, but only if you look for it.
You search, you break your heart, your back, your brain,
and then—and only then—it is handed to you.
— ANNIE DILLARD

I believe that every form of creativity involves a certain amount of such disciplined effort, even if it doesn't actually involve sitting.

First of all, you have to build your skills. Piano players must practice. Ballet dancers must train and rehearse. Painters must sketch and do studies. Writers must draft and read. Engineers must do sample projects. Administrators must study their craft and hone their people skills. There's nothing more frustrating than having a creative idea and not being able to implement it because you lack the practical skills. The hard work of creativity includes the work of getting good enough to do what you really want to do.

It also involves the process of *retrieving* your ideas from your notebooks and your journals. These are not meant to be permanent storage areas, but incubation ovens, constantly bubbling forth with fresh energy. That means you need to have a regular system for pulling your thoughts and ideas out, moving them around, and letting them stimulate further creative ideas. I am constantly browsing through my notebook, tearing out pages, posting them on my bulletin board, pinning them to parts of my easel. Often I will recopy a note or idea into a different form or even have it typed up for editing. In addition, I'll look back through my journals and sketchbooks for insights and images that it may be time to develop.

There's a certain amount of work involved in simply choosing what you want to do: deciding on the problem you want to solve, picking out a subject to paint, determining what medium you want to use to express an idea. This is essentially creative goal setting, and for me it's vital to the creative process. Creating a painting must begin by shaping a sense of where I want to go, even if I end up changing directions in mid-painting.

After the goals are set for a creative endeavor, there's usually some background work to be done. If you want to open a business—and doing that really can be a creative endeavor—you research your markets and draw up a business plan. If you want to bake bread, you pore through recipe books or even research automatic bread bakers. If you want to create a painting, you prepare preliminary sketches and studies, prepare the canvas, lay out your palette, and choose your brushes.

And then, once the homework is done, you really go to work. You flesh out the outline and draft a chapter. You pick up the chunk of wood that will be your sculpture and begin chipping away. You start rehearsals.

And here's the interesting thing, something that many people don't understand: Often you will have proceeded quite a bit with the hands-on process before the real creative inspiration ever hits! Sometimes (I would even say most of the time) you have to begin the work in order for the inspiration to come. The work is what primes the pump, greases the wheels. Sometimes you'll end up throwing away what you first produced or diverging significantly from your first plan, but the work of planning and producing was necessary to get where you needed to go.

Creativity is essentially an act of discovery, an act of faith. You find it as you do it. The painting emerges not only from the original inspiration, but from the accidents of how the paint hits the canvas. The poem emerges from the process of putting words on paper and letting them interact. You discover the best way to run your business by putting your system into place. In short, inspiration comes as you work, so there's no excuse not to get started!

GIVING IT A REST

I have found that there's a paradox to all creative endeavor. You have to work very hard to make it happen—but you can't make it happen simply by working!

The work is necessary, but there comes a point when you have to stop—stop planning, stop processing information, stop developing—and simply do something else while the project continues to develop in the back of your mind.

Every artist I've ever spoken with has experienced this phenomenon. You'll work hard. You'll do your homework. You'll forge a vision and set yourself to the task of making it happen. Perhaps you'll feel you're making progress—the words are flowing, the thoughts are connecting, the brush-strokes seem to be going somewhere. And then, suddenly, you'll hit a snag, or you'll find your interest and energy diverted to something else. The words no longer seem to connect. The painting looks flat and lifeless. You're not sure what to do next.

So you take a break. Perhaps you might say a little prayer and turn the whole situation over to God; I do that all the time. And then you simply go into the kitchen and prepare a snack and wash the dishes. Or you take a walk, or pick up a letter that needs to be answered. You may do a little preliminary work on *another* project.

And then—surprise!—you get another idea, another creative inspiration. While you're in the middle of doing something else, you might feel a key turn over in your brain. A door will open, and suddenly you'll know what to do next. That's when you know you're ready to go back to work.

This process of waiting may take just a few minutes, or it may take longer. You simply have to go on with other activities and trust that the problem will resolve itself without your conscious attention. In my experience as an artist, this "give it a rest" formula has been amazingly dependable. In more than twenty-five years of oil painting, I have yet to throw a painting out because a problem could not be resolved.

What you're doing when you give it a rest, of course, is surrendering the problem to the creative part of you that operates below the conscious level. You're putting the stew on the back burner and letting it simmer, letting the flavors blend into a wonderful, new concoction that even you couldn't have consciously planned.

Here's an interesting thing I've discovered about my own process of back-burner simmering. It works beautifully when I take time away from my work for rest or exercise or mundane chores. But it also works surprisingly well when I plunge myself into another high-energy endeavor or something that fully engages my mind. In other words, my back-burner stew still seems to simmer merrily while I focus on a knotty business problem or become caught up in a mesmerizing novel. Almost always, when I return to my original work, I'll find some creative solutions waiting for me.

But don't get me wrong; I'm not advocating that the best creative work is done in a constant frenzy of plunging from one high-intensity project to the next. Far from it. Creative living at its best involves a rhythm of intense work and not-so-intense work, of times when you do something new and times when you simply enjoy a routine. It involves a balanced mix of the mental and the spiritual and the physical. And that kind of balanced life is not only good for the creative you—it's good for all of you.

Besides, your experience may well be different from mine. You may find, as one of my friends did, that your pot only simmers well when you leave it for tasks that are essentially mundane or routine. Or you may find that your back burner works well when you leave your work for short periods but that your enthusiasm cools when you let a project simmer too long. Only experience can teach you how your creative mind functions best. Nevertheless, I think you'll discover that a simmering back burner is a very dependable resource for creative problem solving.

DON'T LET YOUR CREATIVE PLANT WITHER

Creativity is a powerful, almost irresistible force. The urge to create something new is planted deep within the soul of every person, like a seed under a sidewalk. And like a seed it has remarkable power to sprout and force its way to the surface. This is why you hear singing in prison cells, poems and stories emerging from concentration camps. This is why you see complex murals painted on the walls of burned-out ghetto buildings.

It's not as easy as some might think, in other words, to stifle creativity.

And yet it happens. It happens every day, in wealthy suburbs as well as impoverished neighborhoods. Under certain conditions, the green plant of creativity can wither or even die—and the saddest thing is that we let it happen. We do it to ourselves, and we let others do it to us.

How do we do it? Some of us cripple our creativity with unrealistic expectations and rigid perfectionism. We take to heart the old admonition that "if a thing is worth doing, it's worth doing well," and we judge the creative efforts of ourselves and others before they have a chance to bloom. If we don't understand that the very process of creativity involves risk, failure, trying something, failing, then trying again . . . we'll nip that process in the bud. In any creative endeavor, there has to be room for some creative bumbling—for trying a new pattern that might not work, attempting a new technique that has not been perfected. There has to be some tolerance for a work in progress as well—for an unfinished painting or a half-carved figurine or a new violin technique that might offend perfectionist sensibilities.

It is indeed important to strive for excellence in creative endeavor. It's important to grow in skill, improve technique. But if we make a god of perfection, we risk pushing ourselves into a creative desert. We're afraid to try because we're afraid we won't be good.

A corollary to this overemphasis on excellence is the modern tendency to professionalize creative work. Men and women who in another age would derive great joy from amateur endeavor now are quick to compare their efforts to the work of professionals and to become discouraged. This, I believe, is a direct result of the proliferation of media in everyday life. We are surrounded by high-quality, professionally produced music, drama, and art. And this is good insofar as it adds to our enjoyment in life. But it's bad if it discourages creative effort for the sheer love of it.

Our family is passionately committed to the process of creative endeavor for its own sake. We love to gather around my mother's piano and sing together (often in off-key voices) or listen to the older girls play their practice pieces. We encourage the girls to make up stories, write them down, and illustrate them. And one of our favorite family activities is "skit night," when mom and dad become the audience for makeshift dramatic productions complete with homemade props, enthusiastic stunts, and of course elaborate costumes. In fact, sometimes I suspect that "skit night" is just an excuse to play dress-up. But that's all right, too, because we're not really interested in a professional production, anyway. What we want from these endeavors is the sheer joy of creating.

If a thing is worth doing, it is worth doing badly.
—G. K. CHESTERTON

Another surefire way to wither the green plant of creativity is through hurry and chronic stress. When we are always in a rush, always concerned about doing more and more in less and less time, we almost inevitably fall into the pattern of repeating ourselves, doing the same thing over and over instead of thinking up new possibilities. Up to a point, we may become more *efficient* —more effective in our actions. We may even *feel* more creative, but we'll be considerably less likely to connect ideas and come up with new ones.

Think about it. When you're in a hurry, are you more likely to try a new recipe for dinner or to think of a new system for organizing your drawers? Are you more likely to whistle a new tune or to think of a dynamic title for that novel you've always wanted to write? For most of us, the answer is no.

This principle is well documented in psychological literature. It even has a scientific name, the "Yerkes-Dodson law," which essentially states that people think more creatively when the level of adrenaline in their blood is low and work more effectively when it's high. (At very high adrenaline levels, we panic, and both creativity and effectiveness go out the window!)

Ideally, we were meant to live and work on a cycle of up and down, stress and relaxation, creative thought and effective implementation of ideas. But if we allow ourselves to operate at full speed too much of the time, our creativity is likely to wither.

OUTSIDE THE BOX

Perhaps the most deadly enemy to a creative life is judgmental thinking, the tendency to reject any idea or expression that moves outside the box of what is considered standard or normal. Have you ever stopped to consider how much of your life is directed either by rote habit or the conditioning of others? We all have the tendency to like our comfortable ruts, our stereotyped ways of thinking, our routine approaches to problems. We tend to resist efforts to approach life in any way other than "how we've always done it." We also want to be liked and accepted, which means we may give in too easily to those who insist we must approach our life only along marked paths. In the process, we deny ourselves the opportunity to try new approaches. When we ourselves attempt to venture outside the box, we may experience fear and self-doubt. When other people depart from the obvious, we may criticize them or completely reject them.

I am not really talking here about traditionalism in creative endeavor. I happen to believe, in fact, there is wide berth for creative expression within older, more traditional forms. I personally prefer representational painting as opposed to abstract work, intricately rhyming poetry in place of free verse, tonal music as opposed to dissonant creations. As Robert Frost intimated when he likened free verse to "playing tennis without a net," I have found that the restrictions of traditional forms can actually stimulate more creativity.

But restriction of *attitude*—"You can't do it *that* way!"—is a completely different thing. Creativity tends to wilt in the face of dogmatic dismissal, rigid defense of the status quo, and ignorance of the reality that a given creative destination may be reached in more than one way.

I remember vividly the resentment I felt as an eight-year-old when a certain substitute teacher upbraided me for not preparing a piece of artwork the way she had shown me to do. Even at that age, I tended to see the world in terms of color, not lines, and I just couldn't understand why she insisted that I first draw an outline of an object and then color it in.

As I look back, I can see that this woman probably knew very little about art; she was merely operating from a preconceived notion of how children

should draw. Even now the thought of her harsh criticism, which I sensed even then was based on narrow-mindedness, stings a bit. I feel a tinge of pain on behalf of all the children whose creative spirits have been withered by teachers who insisted there was only one path to creativity. And I regret the loss of their creativity on behalf of a world that desperately needs the input of many minds, many hearts, many different and divergent ways of thinking if it is to improve.

It's a vital thing to remember both as creative people and those who have the opportunity to nurture the creativity in others: *Creativity requires courage!* It takes courage to push ourselves off center, to think in nonstandard ways, to journey outside the ruts. It also takes courage to resist the pressure of those who very much prefer to walk in those ruts. There will always be those whose fierce urge to create gives them the strength to climb out of the box and brave the narrow-mindedness of others. But how much more would creativity flourish in the world if we granted everybody the freedom to bloom?

If you want to live a more creative and joyful life, I urge you to give some attention to climbing outside your box from time to time. If you can do that, chances are you'll be inclined to allow others that privilege as well.

How do you break free of boxed-in thinking? Often you can do it by something as simple as varying your daily routine. Every so often, why not eat salad for breakfast and a banana split for dinner? Go to bed early and wake up early—or do both later than usual. Do your grocery shopping at midnight. Pick up your children from school at noon (with the school's permission) and spend the afternoon at the beach. The point is occasionally to shake yourself free from business as usual, to shake off assumptions about what has to be in order to have more freedom to dream about what could be.

Or here's a fun exercise that can leave you feeling a bit silly but can be very effective in helping you see the inherent strangeness in even familiar objects: Practice looking at the trees, the squirrels, the tricycles and commenting under your breath, "How very interesting!" or "That's amazing!" Try to look at the world you encounter every day as though you had just arrived from another planet or awakened from a long sleep. You'll find you see and appreciate it in a whole new—and probably a more creative—way.

I find that using familiar tools in unfamiliar ways can be especially helpful in pulling me out of my ruts. Occasionally, instead of painting on canvas, I will use ordinary paper mounted on board or even sandpaper glued to a rigid support.

In addition, there's something about limitation that stimulates outside-the-box thinking. I once attempted an entire painting without using white to tint the colors. The process and the effect was bold, vibrant, and very creatively exciting. In the same spirit, you might try writing a poem without using any personal pronouns or baking cookies without using sugar as a sweetener. Try creating a quilt using only circles of fabric—no square shapes whatsoever. Or do a sketch with your nondominant hand. In the very challenge of self-limitation, you'll often find yourself stretching the limit of your creativity and breaking free of the confines of your mental cages. And when you let yourself break out of your box, your creativity can soar.

Prepare a fallow heart to welcome mystery,
water a dormant soul with springs of joy.
Cultivate awe. Plant a seed of hope.
—JOYCE HOLLYDAY

CREATIVE COLLABORATION

The act of creating something new from the raw materials of my life is something that brings me enormous joy. The more deeply involved I become in the act of creation, however, the more I have the sense that the most creative work I do is not really my own—that the ideas and the expression come from outside or beyond me. At times I've had the sense that I was holding the brush but that a power outside myself was guiding my hand. Other times I've found myself looking at a completed painting of mine as if I had never seen it before. "Did I really do that?" I wondered.

Other creative people have told me they've experienced the same phenomenon.

A writer will speak of a "chapter that seemed to write itself."

A businessperson will recall with awe a project where everything just seemed to come together.

A minister will preach a sermon he's preached a dozen times, only to discover, right in the middle of his talk, that the sermon is speaking to *him*.

It doesn't always seem consciously evident, this sense of being a conduit for some larger, more powerful form of creative energy. But sometimes it does. And it is always comforting to remember that, in a way, our creative efforts are truly not our own. When the creative juices are really flowing in any endeavor, there's often the joyful sense of riding a wave. There's a sense of being the tool or a channel or a servant rather than someone in charge. There's the sense that your main job is to get your ego out of the way and let the creativeness flow *through* you rather than *into* you.

Actually, that's exactly what I believe *is* happening.

I believe that what we usually think of as self-expression is really meant to be an act of creative collaboration — almost, if you will, a form of worship. In a way we are offering our minds, our hearts, our bodies as instruments in the divine process of remaking the world.

Perhaps you may think that's a bit grandiose. Perhaps you have a hard time seeing the work of the divine hand in the pot holder you're knitting or the poem you wrote for your sister's birthday.

But don't sell yourself short. Don't sell your creative efforts short. Instead, if you want to live a more joyful life, cultivate a spirit of thankfulness for the incredible privilege that is yours when you create.

Think of it. Whether you're crafting a violin or an oatmeal-box drum for your child, whether you're designing a skyscraper or hammering together a birdhouse, whether you're singing at the opera or in the shower, you still have as a collaborator the creative energy of the universe. You are God's paintbrush, God's pen, God's body to dance upon the earth and bring about the new.

It really is an honor.

More important, it truly is a joy.

When I create, God lights a fresh candle of joy for the world.

LIGHTPOSTS
FOR LIVING

TWELVE

VOYAGING TOWARD DAWN

LIVING IN THE LIGHT OF UNFOLDING MIRACLES

Not fare well,
But fare forward, voyagers.
—T. S. ELIOT

Each of my paintings is a journey. When I embark upon the process of creating, I am never entirely sure where I'll end up.

That doesn't mean I don't know where I'm going or what I want to do. I always begin with a plan in mind, a visualized image of the completed work. And I always proceed through a series of carefully orchestrated stages, working diligently to bring my vision to life. But circumstances can change as the piece on my easel evolves from bare canvas to work-in-progress to finished painting. Sometimes the painting itself seems to have an opinion about what it wants to be, and I've found it's always a good idea to pay attention.

That happened to me just recently as I began work on a peaceful little misty-morning seascape. At least, that's the way I envisioned it—a towering lighthouse presiding over a serene stretch of ocean, all of it shrouded in a silvery haze. It had the potential to be a lovely subject, and as I blocked out the forms and began to develop them I felt the same anticipation I would feel when walking along the beach in the hushed hour before dawn.

As the painting began to take shape, though, some new possibilities seemed to suggest themselves. Somewhere out in that peaceful stretch of ocean I began to get a sense of forms that "wanted" to emerge—some distant islands or points of land with rocky shores and waves beating against them. I could see that these additions would add depth and interest to the painting, so I brushed away some of the mist in the middle distance and added some stronger colors to illuminate the new, distant shores. I knew I was sacrificing my misty morning—the scene now had more of a daylight feel—but the additions were worth it. I liked the mysterious draw of the rocks in the distance.

I continued to work. But then, as I added more layers to soften and blend the colors, I noticed that the overall coloration had warmed even more. What had begun as morning mist and brightened into daylight now had taken on a dusky evening quality. I decided I liked the effect, so I began to enhance it with more layers of glaze. Before long, the sky colors had continued to evolve into a radiant sunset that was actually the centerpiece of the entire painting!

In the course of a few days' development, that painting had not only acquired a new piece of real estate; it had also traveled in time from early morning to full sunset. These developments were a total surprise to me, and yet I knew the painting that emerged was exactly what it should be. As I looked at the piece, I felt the total effect was powerful yet enigmatic, full of energy and movement, yet infused with the sense of stillness and utter peace. In fact, the sense of tranquillity was so strong to me that I decided to title the painting, *The Sea of Tranquillity*.

All that remained then was a few finishing touches—some circling sea-gulls, some reflections on the waves, and finally the ethereal image of a sail-boat silhouetted against the sky, sailing confidently on those peaceful seas into that glorious sunset.

The symbolism of the little boat was no accident. Even as I worked on that painting, as it evolved under my fingertips, I began to see it as a picture of the uncertain but glorious voyage that is every human life. More specifically, that little boat swooping across a peaceful sea under an ever-changing sky is a picture of the kind of life-voyage I want for myself: energetic, adventurous, but also unsinkably serene, no matter what happens along the way.

The months and days are the travelers of eternity.
The years that come and go are also voyagers.
—MATSUO BASHŌ

What Do You Expect?

What's the secret of such serene sailing? I think the answer lies to a great extent in what you expect from the work-in-progress that is your life.

A life, after all, is seldom an uneventful sail from one point to another. You may plan carefully, chart your course, stock just the right provisions . . . and run into high seas or get caught in the doldrums. Chances are you'll have to make some navigational corrections along the way or even some radical changes of direction, and there's still no guarantee that you'll end up where you expected to be.

You may plan to be an architect and end up being an accountant. Or you may start out to be an accountant, take up drawing as a hobby, then go back to school to be an architect!

Perhaps you'll long for children and end up single, or you'll swear you don't want children and end up with a houseful.

You may aspire to be an Olympic athlete, only to sustain an injury and be forced to retire from sports—or perhaps you'll develop an even more absorbing interest in traveling and end up in the Peace Corps instead of the Games.

You might even end up like a friend

of a friend of mine, who passionately desired to be a writer and to live and work in the mountains. On a summer trip to Ireland, she met the man of her dreams . . . and ended up happily married to a Dutchman, living and raising her family in one of the flattest, lowest-lying places on earth! The interesting thing is that living as an expatriate helped her find work translating books. From there she became an editor and from there she obtained some contracts to write books. And to meet with her editor and put her first novel into final form, she had to go . . . to the mountains!

The simple fact is that life, like the process of painting and the course of a sea voyage, is unpredictable, and we human beings are seldom granted access to the grand plan of the universe. If you place your trust in things working out just the way you planned, you'll probably end up disappointed and even bitter. If you give up entirely on trusting and planning, you may well end up stagnated or in despair.

But here's another possibility: Instead of laying down a list of expectations for what your life *should* be, you can participate in the ongoing discovery of what your life *was meant* to be.

In other words, you can learn to trust in the principle of unfolding miracles—and in the unfolding miracle that is your life.

What do I mean by unfolding miracle? A more old-fashioned word for it is *providence*. It simply means that we are provided with what we need, when we need it—but usually not before, and not without our participation.

This is the way I believe our life was meant to progress. It's not a cut-and-dried plan, not a seat-of-the-pants scramble, but an ongoing, interactive process. We sail forward as best we can, we pay attention to the condition of the seas, and along the way we employ our very best seamanship. But even as we go, we know there will always be a star to steer by, always a lighthouse or a buoy to head us away from total shipwreck, even a storm or two to nudge us off the course we thought we wanted and onto the course that will take us home.

Something amazing happens when you learn to take this view of what you do and what happens to you. Trusting in the principle of unfolding miracles sets you free from the need to have all the answers, to provide for every possibility. You're freed from the exhausting responsibility of having to be in complete control of what happens to you. You learn the amazing liberty of having faith that everything really will be all right. It's an exciting, open-ended, inherently joyful but also amazingly peaceful way to live.

What Is a Miracle?

But does this all sound just a bit esoteric, a tad too spiritual for everyday life? Perhaps I should clarify what I mean by miracles.

When I speak of miracles, I don't necessarily mean that the heavens part, that the laws of nature are suspended, that problems and illnesses disappear and money and opportunities appear out of the blue. Rather, the unfolding miracles that determine the course of our lives take the form of natural circumstances with perfect timing—the phone call from a friend that comes just when you are about to give up, a neighbor's donation of a secondhand washing machine that meets a long-standing need, the chance conversation in the grocery store checkout line that results in a new relationship or a new career.

Unless you have your eyes open, you might not even recognize these occurrences for the miracles they are. But learning to recognize the miracles that shape your life is a powerful key to maintaining daily joy.

Here's an example of the kind of miracle I mean. As a young boy living in a single-parent home, I felt the need to contribute to the family income, so I found a job at the local sign shop. My first day at work I met a man named Charles Bell, who was to shape my future significantly. Charlie was a bit of an eccentric who had worked a variety of jobs over the years—sign work, ship design, book illustration, you name it. He was also a tremendously hard-working, thorough man, and he was willing to take me under his wing. Looking back, I can see that Charles Bell was instrumental in teaching me the discipline and the work ethic that have helped turn my dreams of an art career into reality.

Now, the simple fact of a boy getting a job and finding a mentor might not seem miraculous in itself. But consider the timing: I was thirteen years old, growing up without a father in the home. To me, the provision of a strong male role model who could teach me the values I needed as well as many of the basics of art technique qualifies as a true miracle. Without that particular divine coincidence, my life would probably have turned out quite differently. I have no problem at all believing that my sign shop job and my relationship with Charlie were truly providential in my life.

And here's a similar well-timed circumstance that I now look back on and recognize as a miracle. I was fifteen and living with my family in Placerville, California, a small mountain town with little or no focus on the arts. I knew I wanted to be an artist, although I really didn't have much of a clue how that could happen in my life. That's when I found out that we were going to have a new neighbor, a man named Glenn Wessels, who was renovating an old barn just two hundred feet from our house.

Here's the amazing part: This man was a nationally known artist. Before his retirement, he had been head of the art department at the University of California as well as an established art critic and scholar on the subject of fine art. He was one of the nation's top experts in the traditions of representa-tional painting, and after his retirement he had decided to move away from the city. He just happened to choose our town and our street as the place to establish a new home and studio. Miraculous.

Even then, that circumstance felt like a divine intervention to me, a con-firmation that art was to be my life's work. I showed up on his doorstep and volunteered to help him in his studio in return for lessons. At first he was gra-cious but not really interested. A year later, after being injured in a jeep acci-dent, he realized he needed the help.

Over the next few years, that studio became my second home. I can still smell that pungent atmosphere of stale coffee and turpentine. And in my imagination I can still sit beside that great man as he taught me not *how* to paint, but *why* to paint. Glenn Wessels poured the accumulated wisdom of a lifetime into my eager young mind. Under his influence, I came to appreciate the grand heritage of painting and to understand that art has a meaning, a purpose. In many significant ways, Glenn Wessels helped me forge my philosophy and my motivation as both an artist and a human being.

Once again, there was nothing really so unusual about an old man's decision to retire to a small town or his needing help around the studio. But to me, as I examine the astounding coincidence of all the factors that combined to give a restless teenager in a small country town the chance for contact with the larger worlds of art and education through the vehicle of a lonely, retired college professor, it seems nothing short of a miracle. And I could name a hundred more examples of times when my life unfolded in ways that I can now see as miraculous. Happy accidents, remarkable coincidences, and even painful experiences have nudged me in the direction I needed to go, year by year. I have observed with awe as circumstances combined with my own choices (even my own mistakes) to bring me where I am today.

HAVING FAITH

But my purpose in recounting these few examples is not really to draw attention to the many miraculous things that I have experienced.

My purpose is to suggest that there's a similar process going on in your own life, whether you can see it or not. Your life really is part of an unfolding plan, a charted voyage, an exquisitely executed work of art. Every circumstance in your life, every event that occurs is moving you a little closer to your final destination. Every response you make adds another brushstroke to the final picture.

Your life has meaning and beauty, and you are not in it alone. If you can believe that, you'll have reason enough for traveling joyfully and peacefully.

> *Hope is hearing the melody of the future. Faith is to dance it.*
> —RUBEM A. ALVES

But that's really the rub, isn't it? *How* do you learn to trust that you'll be taken care of, that the miracles will kick in when you need them? Where do

you come up with the kind of faith that keeps you sailing serenely, no matter what your circumstances?

The truest, most basic answer to that question is both supremely challenging and profoundly simple: You learn by doing it. You learn to trust in miracles by sailing forward daily with a growing awareness that your needs will be met.

You don't have to be completely sure of yourself, completely confident in your beliefs. You don't even have to feel particularly trustful. You simply have to summon the courage to untie those ropes and push off from shore. When you encounter a hitch in your plans—a professional setback, a time of marital stress, a physical illness, or just a sense of being on hold, you do what you humanly can and then watch for the miracle that lies hidden behind the unexpected change in course.

I promise you, it's there. Perhaps you'll fail spectacularly at one job, only to find satisfaction in a completely different one. Perhaps you'll learn from your setback and be able to help others with a similar challenge. Perhaps your marital stress will lead you to a stronger foundation for your relationship. Perhaps a time of illness will teach you to savor life more. Whatever your miracle, it will give you the opportunity once more to move forward in faith.

That's really what faith is, in fact. As I see it, faith is more than just belief. It's really a form of courage. Faith is the willingness to act upon your sense of what you think lies behind the external circumstances. It's the choice to sail forward before you are completely sure why you are going through what you are going through, before you are completely confident you can trust the final outcome.

Again, it's a dynamic process. You move forward on the best evidence you have, and it is that very process of moving forward that makes your faith possible.

That description may sound more heroic than you want to be. But faith in yourself, faith in your future, faith in God's providence is really not all that challenging a proposition. Once you get in the habit of watching for miracles, it feels like the most natural thing in the world.

It may help to keep in mind that you make faith assumptions all the time. You get in a car, trusting that it will take you where you want to go, and most of the time it does. You walk across your kitchen floor, assuming it will hold you up, and unless the termites have moved excessively fast, you won't be disappointed. It's certainly *possible* for a floor to fall through. It's even more possible for a car to break down or not to start. But you've learned that faith assumptions like these are really a good bet. Besides, if you spent all your time questioning the trustworthiness of these things, you would never go anywhere.

So here's the bottom line: You learn faith by acting in faith. You learn to trust in miracles by watching for them. You learn to sail serenely by untying the ropes and setting sail.

Even so, there are some things you can do to make these learning processes a little faster and easier. You can take some specific steps to become more aware of the miracles in your life and to take advantage of the exciting process of divine providence as it unfolds.

THE NOVEL OF YOUR LIFE

Have you ever thought of your life as a mystery novel? As a situation comedy? An epic movie adventure? A heart-wrenching memoir?

Your life might not be ready for print, but it still has a story to tell—and the best person to tell it to is yourself. Looking back over the course of your life is the best way I know to begin to discern the miraculous circumstances that have brought you where you are today and to begin trusting the miracles that will take you into the future.

How do you tell your story to yourself? The simplest, most effective way I know is to write it down. You don't have to prepare a full-fledged memoir or autobiography. You can simply set yourself the goal of writing a ten-page summary of where your life has brought you so far.

Here's a good place to start. Find a legal pad (or sit down at your computer) and scrawl out a one-page account of your earliest clear and full memory. Who was there? What happened? How old were you? Don't just sketch in a bare outline. Try to write down specific details—sights, sounds, smells, feelings. Make the picture as vivid as possible, without worrying too much about what may be important or relevant.

Chances are, as you explore that specific memory, more memories will occur to you. Keep a separate page handy to jot them down—your first Christmas, the puppy you had as a child, your friend who moved away, the teacher who helped you understand math. You may recall people you haven't seen in years, places you had all but forgotten, events that have totally slipped your mind. The very act of writing down your memories is almost guaranteed to trigger more and more memories.

Honor your own stories and tell them too.
The tales may not seem very important, but they are
what . . . makes each of us who we are.
— MADELEINE L'ENGLE

Next, on a new sheet, you might want to begin a general outline of the events of your life—where you lived, where you went to school, how the dates of your experience coincided with the dates of history. Where were you when John F. Kennedy was assassinated? When Neil Armstrong walked on the moon? When the Berlin Wall came down? Write down dates that you remember, events that loom as important in your mind. Write down addresses and names. These concrete facts are part of the picture, too. They'll help you put your more subjective memories in perspective.

After you've collected enough random memories or the flow of remembering has started to ebb, and after you've sketched in a general outline, go back and read what you have written so far. Look for patterns and watershed events, the relationships and occurrences that determined the direction of your life. What experiences gave you encouragement and urged you on? Which ones made you cautious or afraid? Who helped you? Who influenced you?

Consider the ways you responded to events as well, for this will be clearer in retrospect. Look for times when you have learned from mistakes and times when have you repeated the same mistakes over and over. Consider what you regret and what you are proud of. Look for patterns in your responses.

Most of all, try to find those points in your life where what has happened and what you have done converged to move you forward and significantly shape the person you have become. Those are your miracles! Thank God for them, even for those that seem to have moved you in a negative direction. Remember that your life story isn't finished yet—you can't presume to know how it will come out. You never know when what looks like a curse might turn out to be a blessing.

The process of telling your story doesn't have to be completed in a day or even a week. It may take you months to gather your memories and pare them down into ten pages of the most significant events. You may even decide the process is so interesting that you want to write more than ten pages.

Telling your story can be enormously helpful, but there is no law that insists your life story has to be *written*. If you are more visually oriented, perhaps you would prefer to sketch your memories or to prepare an album of selected photographs. (One creative woman I know, a teacher of young children, created a pop-up book to tell part of her story.) Perhaps you'd prefer to speak your recollections into an audio or video recorder. Or you could relate your memories to your children out loud. Keep in mind that your point is to look at your past from a fresh perspective, learning to see and appreciate the patterns of providence that have shaped your life.

While you're in the process, I suggest giving yourself some inspiration by reading and listening to the stories of other lives. Read biographies of people you admire. (My copy of Norman Rockwell's *My Adventures as an Illustrator* is well worn from repeated readings.) Good fiction, too, can hold up a helpful mirror to the process of telling your life story. And one of your best sources of both information and inspiration is the members of your own family. Ask questions of those who are older, especially your parents and grandparents. Interview them and encourage them to tell you their own stories. The act of listening will strengthen your relationships while helping you understand the unfolding of your own life.

Finally, after you've listened to stories of the past and told some of your own, I urge you to continue the process of storytelling on a regular basis. Viewing the progress of your life from a distance, as a filmmaker or writer might, is an invaluable tool in discerning the presence of your personal miracles. Those events that seem definitive occurred for a reason. Each turning point in your life is the key to a new direction, each closed door a chance to explore new options.

GO DEEP

Even as you're in the process of discerning the patterns in your life, I encourage you to seek the underlying meaning of the events. You were made for more than surface living, so don't be afraid to go deep, to dig out a spiritual reality that might not be readily discernible at first glance.

You don't have to believe in God to do this. You don't really have to believe in anything at all. All you have to do is open your mind to the possibility that there is more to life than what you already know, more to reality than what you can verify by the senses. You need to be willing to ask the questions, then to expend some time and energy looking for the answers.

In a sense, spiritual seeking is like going into training. You don't get into physical shape by wishing you were a better athlete, and you don't get into better spiritual condition by harboring some vague spiritual yearnings. If you want to get a better sense of the miracle that is your life, it's advisable to spend some time exercising your spiritual muscles through a process of practice and training.

The best way I know to begin (or renew) a spiritual search is simply through a daily quiet time. Depending on your religious background (or lack of it), you may want to meditate or repeat a simple prayer or speak to God from your heart. Some people kneel. Some people stand, or sit with their legs crossed. Some people read inspirational literature; others write in their journals. One woman I heard of simply sat on a piano bench for fifteen minutes a day, timing herself with a kitchen timer.

Don't worry if a million distracting thoughts crowd into your mind. (They will.) Simply take them one by one and lay them aside. Tell them "later." Do whatever you can to quiet your spirit, and then wait. If you do this simple thing over a significant period of time (say, two to four weeks), I'm convinced you'll begin to experience just how real your spiritual life can be.

Another practice that many have found helpful in their seeking is to go on a retreat. This simply means getting away from your regular activities for a day or two and spending some time alone. Think of it as a spiritual vacation, an opportunity to break loose from daily preoccupations and concentrate on the deeper meaning of your life. You can call a local church or religious organization for information regarding retreats being sponsored locally, but I have found that a simple tent beneath the stars or even a quiet hotel room will do as well. You can even make a retreat at home if you can manage to be alone and ignore the TV and phone!

What do you do during this set-apart time? Whatever you are led to do.

Some people read. Some people write. Some people take long walks. One man I know fell deeply in love with his God through spending two weeks digging out a basement by hand. What really matters is not what you do, but the fact that you use the activity as a tool for delving more deeply into your life and exploring its underlying meaning. As you do, you'll no doubt acquire some fresh perspective on the ongoing course of your existence.

One of the most helpful ways to dig deeper into your life is to expose yourself to people of faith, people who are farther along on the journey than you are. You can do this through books, through magazines, through talking to other people. Do you know someone whose life exudes the kind of joy you would like for yourself? Ask that person to tell you his or her story. Go to the library and seek out books with spiritual themes. Most of all, spend regular time with scriptures or holy writings that have meaning to you. My own personal Christian faith has been bolstered time and time again through my readings in the Bible, both the Hebrew Scriptures and the New Testament.

As you read and spend time alone, try this as an exercise: Write a statement affirming what you believe. Don't write what you think you *should* believe or what you *want* to believe. Try to be as honest as possible in describing exactly where you are.

You may only be able to say, for example, that you believe there is more to life than meets the eye. Or you may be able to affirm that someone made you, or that you believe there is a God but you don't feel much personal involvement with that fact. Whatever you can honestly affirm, write it down. Perhaps you can begin each statement of faith with "I believe." Then fold your finished statement, put it in an envelope, date it, and set it aside with a prayer: "Please teach me more." Two years from now, you may be surprised at how much you have grown.

Finally, whatever else you do, practice looking for touches of the divine in your everyday life. This is the best way I know to teach yourself to pick up on unfolding miracles. Look for the eternal in the faces of children, in leaves and stones and other wonders of nature, in the intricate tapestry of daily events. Keep your eyes and heart open for the signs of spiritual reality hiding behind a familiar disguise.

You will begin to see these signs, and they will change your life. All you have to do is keep looking—digging a little deeper—and they will find you.

KEEP YOUR HOPE ALIVE

I like to think of hope as a guiding light for the human heart. It is the
quality that will help you find your way through dark and stormy nights,

through foggy and confusing days. It's the best antidote to fear and despair, the quality of positive expectation that lets you see past the place where you are to the better place where you can be. It's one of the best ways I know to shed light on the process of unfolding miracles—and it's part of the ongoing miracle itself.

In my observation, human beings can survive almost any circumstance except the complete loss of hope. Fortunately, hope is a very resilient quality. It can keep on shining for a long time, even in the darkest conditions. Its stubborn gleam has been seen in ghetto apartments, in concentration camps, in shelters for battered women, wandering the city streets and rural lanes. Its beautiful light can point the way out of the most intolerable situation.

Best of all, hope is a renewable quality. Its batteries can be recharged, and its beam can be strengthened. Even when you feel your hope light dimming, there are usually simple steps you can take to keep it shining brightly in your life.

How do you keep your hope light charged? One of the most basic ways is to surround yourself with positive, uplifting people. Hope is highly contagious; you can catch it from hopeful traveling companions. Seek them out and make them part of your life.

Here's another way for building hope that might not have occurred to you: Take care of your body. You might be surprised at how effective adequate exercise, proper nutrition, and sufficient sleep can be in helping you maintain an attitude of positive expectation. Every year, medical science seems to learn something new about the relationship between mind, body, and spirit and one thing that's becoming clear is that the chemicals in the brain are intricately related to the experience of hope. Keeping your body running the way it was supposed to can be enormously effective in lifting your spirits.

To live joyfully is to live in hope.
— JUDITH BRUDER

Solving a nagging problem is also a surprising but dependable way to build up your hope reserves. Often, if you take an inventory of the circumstances in your life that seem to drain your hope, you'll discover that a few chronic dilemmas are to blame. Try isolating one of these and taking steps to solve it. Write a letter asking forgiveness. Make a visit to heal a relationship. Change your job. Change your diet. Move the sofa. You might be surprised at how hopeful you'll feel once you've taken care of even a single nagging difficulty.

In my life I often find that certain types of work—filing paperwork, for example—can build up and become a nagging distraction. When this happens, I make a "date" with the problem. I set a specific time on my calendar to address it and refuse to work on other priorities until the task is done. The relief from lifting this minor burden fuels extra efficiency and lightheartedness throughout the whole day, and I am free to focus on other challenges more effectively. I certainly feel more hopeful.

And here's yet another surprising hope builder: Study some history. Read a social history of the Middle Ages, or rent the PBS video account of the Civil War, or visit a nearby pioneer museum, or interview a Vietnam War veteran. Remind yourself as you read and listen that both joy and pain are part of the human condition, but that the human race has survived for a remarkably long time. Chances are, it will continue. Chances are, you'll be able to move forward as well.

ᴡ

VOYAGING FORWARD

When you live in the light of unfolding miracles, there is always a future, always a hope. You can count on the fact that your life will change, and you can trust that, as it does, everything will work out as it should. As you explore the story of your life, dig deep to discover the faith that moves you forward. Shining the beam of hope into your times of darkness, you'll learn to sail with more confidence.

The sailing won't always be smooth. Undoubtedly, you will encounter some rough seas. A storm or two will cloud the horizon from time to time. But eventually, you'll find, the storms will pass. The rough seas will calm. Unexpected changes in course may well lead to exciting, unexplored possibilities. Even better, having gone through the storm and darkness, you will find you've become a far better sailor. Learning to navigate by faith and to trust in a dependable providence, you have become a person of unsinkable serenity.

You still won't know exactly where life's going to take you. You may start out on a misty morning and end up sailing into a gorgeous sunset. Or you may take a completely different tack and end up sailing directly into the dawn—but that's just one more reason for joy.

Bon voyage!

When I see my life as a series of unfolding miracles,
I'll always sail forth with hope, tranquillity,
and joy in my heart.

LIGHTPOSTS
FOR LIVING

AFTERWORD

LET YOUR LIGHT SHINE

Let your light so shine before men,
that they may see your good works . . .
—THE BOOK OF MATTHEW

For quite some time now, I have been described as "The Painter of Light." Whenever I hear those words, I feel an inner challenge to live up to everything this phrase implies.

In my deepest heart of hearts, I *want* to be a painter of light. I *want* to create works that glow with lasting beauty and positive inspiration. I *want* to use my paintings to share the values I believe in: faith, hope, joy, peacefulness, family, beauty.

For years, my prayer has been that somehow my work would be used to shine the light of encouragement and inspiration into the world around me. Today I stand in awe of the many ways that God has answered that prayer—opening doors for me to share my art with others, using the paintings themselves to encourage those who see them.

The most amazing thing is that he chose me to be a part of it. Despite the limitations of my family background, despite my less-than-perfect childhood, despite my many personal shortcomings, God has positioned me perfectly for the unique task I was called to do. For reasons that to me are often unclear but always miraculous, God chose me.

And do you know what? God chose *you*, too!

I believe that each of us, out of the billions of souls on our planet, has been uniquely prepared for the calling that is our life. Despite our human failings, we each have a purpose.

And I believe that each of us, in our own way, is an artist.

You may not be skilled with paints and brushes, but you are still involved in creating an intricate, beautifully crafted work of art: your life. With every moment that you experience, every choice you make, you are adding brushstrokes to the canvas. More important, you are determining what kind of message your artwork will convey to the world.

Are you painting a dark, gloomy nocturne, full of sadness and bitterness? You can choose to do that if you wish.

Are you creating a flat, zestless still life? You can choose that as well.

Is your life a formless collection of random strokes, dabbed on without thought or purpose? That, too, is a possibility.

Or are you preparing a life-canvas that is balanced and beautiful, full of meaning and touched with radiant light—one that not only brings you joy but that also serves as an encouragement to all who see it? Such a choice, too, is within your reach. And what you choose is important, because more is at stake than your own happiness.

I believe we all have a greater purpose to our lives than merely existing day to day—a greater purpose, even, than filling our own lives with light and joy. Each of us, in our own unique way, is called to *let our light shine*. The unique, one-of-a-kind canvas of our existence is meant to be an inspiration to others—a true joy to behold and a heaven-sent blessing to those we meet and to the world around us.

It's the highest calling any of us have in life: making the world a little brighter because of the way we paint our days and hours and months and years.

It's no secret that darkness is in plentiful supply in our world today— hatred, ignorance, despair abound. We all have times when we find ourselves stumbling in the dark. But we all have the capacity, through the way we respond to the world and through the choices we make, to push the darkness back a little. We always have the opportunity, in the words of the old saying, to light a candle rather than curse the darkness.

In this book I have attempted to describe a few simple ways you can bring more light into the work-in-progress that is your life. These principles are not difficult, and they are available to anyone. I believe that making a few basic choices can fill any life with golden joy, with childlike enthusiasm, with balance and simplicity. With a little effort our lives can glow with optimism and beauty, with the comforts of home and the enjoyment of selfless service to others. Any life can radiate with thankfulness and romantic zest, with creativity, energy, and a peaceful, trusting faith. *Your* life can radiate the kind of light that truly makes a difference in the world.

The influence a work of art can have is limited by its physical existence. If at some point the painting or its reproductions are gone, its influence is gone as well. But a human life is a work of art that can reach eternity. Each life has the ability to touch other lives, which in turn touches yet more lives. And so, person by person, generation by generation, a world and a future are shaped.

It seems pretty obvious: If enough people filled their lives with light, the world would be a pretty bright place. But if even one person lives more radiantly and joyfully, the world will still be brighter than it was!

I'm sure we could all agree that the world has enough darkness in it already. Now it's time for your decision. Will you be a part of the darkness or a part of the light? As a fellow human being, I encourage you: For your own sake, for the sake of others, for the sake of the world . . .

Let Your Light Shine!

SOURCES OF LIGHT

Light comes into our lives from many sources, including those whose words spark our imaginations and inspire our ideas. In that spirit, I am indebted to the following people (and a few literary characters) from whose widsom I have quoted in this book:

Alcott, Louisa May. *Little Women or Meg, Jo, Beth and Amy.* New York and Avenel, N.J.: Random House Value Publishing, 1987, 14.

Allen, Elizabeth Akers. In *Bartlett's Familiar Quotations,* 16th edition. Ed. by Justin Kaplan. Boston: Little, Brown and Company, 1992, 516:13.

Alves, Rubem A. *Tomorrow's Child: Imagination, Creativity, and the Rebirth of Culture.* New York: Harper & Row, 1972, 195.

Auntie Mame: Jerome Lawrence and Robert E. Lee. *Auntie Mame.* New York: Vanguard Press, 1957, 37. Play is based on Patrick Dennis's best selling fictionalized memoir of the same name. Minor adaption is from Betty Comden and Adolph Green's screenplay adaption for the 1958 film version of the play.

Barrie, J. M. "What Every Woman Knows" In *The Plays of J. M. Barrie.* New York: Charles Scribner's Sons, 1928, 353.

Bashō, Matsuo. In *Bartlett's Familar Quotations,* 282:11.

Boone, Debby. In *Counting Blessings* by Debby Boone and illustrated by Gabriel Ferrer. Copyright © 1998 by Resi, Inc.: Eugene, Oregon: Harvest House Publishers, 1998. Used by permission.

Bruder, Judith. *Convergence: A Reconciliation of Judaism and Christianity in the Life of One Woman.* New York: Doubleday, 1993, 5.

Buechner, Frederick. *Listening to Your Life: Daily Meditations with Frederick*

Buechner. Comp. by George Connor. San Francisco: HarperSanFrancisco, 1992, 287.

Chesterton, G. K. In *The Oxford Dictionary of Quotations*, 148:10

Cloninger, Claire. *A Place Called Simplicity.* Eugene, Ore.: Harvest House Publishers, 1993, 72.

Coleridge, Samuel Taylor. In *Bartlett's Familiar Quotations*, 383:10.

Dillard, Annie. "The Writing Life." In *Pilgrim at Tinker Creek, An American Childhood, The Writing Life.* Camp Hill, Pa.: Book-of-the-Month Club, Inc., by arrangement with Harper & Row, 1990, 75.

Ecclesiastes 11:7 and 9:10. *The Transformer: Holy Bible, New King James Version.* Nashville: Thomas Nelson, 1985. The New King James Version is copyright © 1982 by Thomas Nelson, Inc. Subsequent references to this source will be designated NKJV.

Eliot, T. S. In *Bartlett's Familiar Quotations*, 671:17.

Emerson, Ralph Waldo. In Luci Swindoll, *You Bring the Confetti.* Waco, Tex. World Books, 1986, 134.

Eeyore: A. A. Milne. *Winnie the Pooh In the World of Pooh: The Complete Winnie-the-Pooh and The House at Pooh Corner.* New York: E. P. Dutton, 1985, 113.

Godek, Gregory J. P. *1001 Ways to Be Romantic.* Weymouth, Mass.: Casablanca Press, Inc., 1991, 1.

Hammarskjöld, Dag. *Markings.* Tr. by Leif Sjöberg and W. H. Auden. New York: Alfred A. Knopf, 1964, 118.

Hollyday, Joyce. "Living the Word: Reflections on the Revised Common Lectionary." *Sojourners: Faith, Politics, and Culture 23*, no. 10 (Dec 94/Jan 95): 30.

Huffman, Carolyn. *Bloom Where You Are.* Waco, Tex.: Word Books, 1976.

Keats, John. In *Bartlett's Familiar Quotations*, 414:9.

Kingma, Daphne Rose. "Introduction." *Random Acts of Kindness.* Comp. by the editors of Conari Press. Berkeley, Calif.: Conari Press, 1993, 1.

L'Engle, Madeleine. "Tell Me a Story." *Victoria*, April 1995, 32.

Letts, Billie. *Where the Heart Is.* New York: Warner Books, 1995, 18.

Matthew 5:16, *NKJV.*

Mains, Karen Burton. *Lonely No More: A Woman's Journey to Personal, Marital, and Spiritual Healing.* Dallas: Word Publishing, 1993, 49.

Miller, Calvin. *The Book of Seven Truths: A Tale of Hope and Restoration.* San Francisco: HarperSanFrancisco, 1997, 94.

Milton, John. In *The Oxford Dictionary of Quotations,* 341:8 and 351:7.

Moran, Victoria. *Shelter for the Spirit: Create Your Own Haven in a Hectic World.* New York: HarperPerennial, 1998, 26 and 155.

Morris, William. In *The Oxford Dictionary of Quotations,* 358:14.

Navajo Night Chant. In *Bartlett's Familiar Quotations,* 787:10.

Osgood, Don. *Listening for God's Silent Language: Hearing God Speak in the Unexpected Places of Life.* Minneapolis: Bethany House Publishers, 1995, 26.

Paul the Apostle. 1 Corinthians 6:12. *The Holy Bible: New Revised Standard Version.* New York: Oxford University Press, 1989. The New Revised Standard Version is copyright © 1989 by the Division of Christian Education for the National Council of the Churches of Christ in the United States of America.

Parkhurst, Charles. *The Home Book of Quotations: Classical and Modern,* 10th edition. Selected and arranged by Burton Stevenson. New York: Dodd, Mead and Company, 1967, 904:14.

Philippians 4:8, *NKJV.*

Quindlen, Anna. In Sarah Ban Breathnach, *Simple Abundance: A Daybook of Comfort and Joy.* New York: Warner Books, 1995.

Reeve, Christopher. *Still Me.* New York: Random House, 1998, 275.

Rosetti, Christina Georgina. In *The Encyclopedia of Religious Quotations.* Ed. and comp. by Frank S. Mead. Westwood, N.J.: Fleming H. Revell Company, 1965, 440.

Saint-Exupéry, Antoine de. *The Little Prince.* New York: Harcourt, Brace and World, 1943, dedication and 51.

Sayers, Dorothy L. *Gaudy Night.* New York: Harper & Row, Perennial Library, 1986, 221.

Shaker hymn. In *Rise Up Singing: the Group-Singing Song Book.* Ed. by Peter Blood and Annie Patterson, Bethlehem, Pa.: Sing Out Corporation,

1988, 1992, 47. Minor changes in punctuation have been made in this volume.

Shedd, Charlie, and Martha Shedd. *Celebration in the Bedroom*. Waco, Tex.: Word Books, 1985, 13.

Stevenson, Robert Louis. In *The Oxford Dictionary of Quotations*, 522:22.

Thoreau, Henry David. *The Portable Thoreau*. Ed. by Carl Bode. New York: The Viking Press, 1947, 844.

Van Dyke, Henry. "Home Song." In *The Works of Henry Van Dyke*, vol. 9: *Poems I*. Avalon Edition. New York: Charles Scribner's Sons, 1921, 217.

Wilder, Thornton. *Our Town: A Play in Three Acts*. New York: Harper & Row, 1957, 45.

Wordsworth, William. In *Bartlett's Familiar Quotations*, 373:3.

Wright, Wendy M. (ch.2) "In the Circle of a Mother's Arms." *Weavings: A Journal of the Christian Spiritual Life 3*, no. 1 (January/February 1988):16.

—. (ch. 7) *The Vigil: Keeping Watch in the Season of Christ's Coming*. Nashville: Upper Room Books, 1992, 34.